IN THE PECOS COUNTRY

LIEUTENANT R. H. JAYNE

[pseudonym of Edward Sylvester Ellis (1840-1916)]

1st WORLD LIBRARY
Literary Society

In the Pecos Country

Lieutenant R. H. Jayne

© 1st World Library, 2007
PO Box 2211
Fairfield, IA 52556
www.1stworldlibrary.com
First Edition

LCCN: 2007930815

Softcover ISBN: 978-1-4218-4857-0
Hardcover ISBN: 978-1-4218-4760-3
eBook ISBN: 978-1-4218-4954-6

Purchase *"In the Pecos Country"*
as a traditional bound book at:
www.1stWorldLibrary.com/purchase.asp?ISBN=978-1-4218-4857-0

1st World Library is a literary, educational organization
dedicated to:

- Creating a free internet library of downloadable ebooks

- Hosting writing competitions and offering book publishing
  scholarships.

Interested in more 1st World Library books? contact:
literacy@1stworldlibrary.com
Check us out at: www.1stworldlibrary.com

1ˢᵗ World Library Literary Society

Giving Back to the World

"If you want to work on the core problem, it's early school literacy."

- James Barksdale, former CEO of Netscape

"No skill is more crucial to the future of a child, or to a democratic and prosperous society, than literacy."

- Los Angeles Times

"Literacy... means far more than learning how to read and write... The aim is to transmit... knowledge and promote social participation."

- UNESCO

"Literacy is not a luxury, it is a right and a responsibility. If our world is to meet the challenges of the twenty-first century we must harness the energy and creativity of all our citizens."

- President Bill Clinton

"Parents should be encouraged to read to their children, and teachers should be equipped with all available techniques for teaching literacy, so the varying needs and capacities of individual kids can be taken into account."

- Hugh Mackay

CHAPTER I

A WARNING

In the valley of the Rio Pecos, years ago, an attempt at founding a settlement was made by a number of hardy and daring New Englanders, whose leader was a sort of Don Quixote, who traveled hundreds of miles, passing by the richest land, the most balmy climate, where all were protected by the strong arm of law, for the sake of locating where the soil was only moderate, the climate no better, and where, it may be said, the great American government was as powerless to protect its citizens as was a child itself. The Rio Pecos, running through New Mexico and Texas, drains a territory which at that time was one of the most dangerous in the whole Indian country; and why these score or more of families should have hit upon this spot of all others, was a problem which could never be clearly solved.

The head man, Caleb Barnwell, had some odd socialistic theories, which, antedating as they did the theories of Bellamy, were not likely to thrive very well upon New England soil, and he pursuaded his friends to go with him, under the belief that the spot selected was one where they would have full opportunity to increase and multiply, as did the Mormons during their early days at Salt Lake. Then, too, there was some reason to suspect that rumors had reached the ears of Barnwell of the existence of gold and silver along this river, and it was said that he had hinted as much to those whom he believed he could trust. Be that as it may, the score of families reached the valley of the Upper Pecos in due time, and the settlement was begun and duly christened New Boston.

"How long do yer s'pose you folks are goin' to stay yer? Why, just long enough for Lone Wolf to hear tell that you've arriv, and he'll down here and clear you out quicker'n lightning."

This was the characteristic observation made by the old scout, hunter and guide, Sut Simpson, as he reined up his mustang to chat awhile with the new-comers, whom he looked upon as the greatest lunk-heads that he had ever encountered in all of his rather eventful experience. He had never seen them before; but he did not care for that, as he had the frankness of a frontiersman and never stood upon ceremony in the slightest degree.

"Did you ever hear tell of Lone Wolf?" he continued, as a group, including nearly the entire population, gathered about the veteran of the plains. "I say, war any of you ever introduced to that American gentleman?"

He looked around, from face to face, but no one responded. Whenever he fixed his eye upon any individual, that one shook his head to signify that he knew nothing of the Apache chief whose name he had just mentioned.

"What I meant to say," he continued, "is that any of you have got any yearnin' toward Lone Wolf, feeling as if your heart would break if you didn't get a chance to throw your arms about him, why, you needn't feel bad, *'cause you'll get the chance*."

Lieutenant R. H. Jayne

There was a significance in these words which made it plain to every one of those who were looking up in the scarred face of the hunter. As they were spoken, he winked one of his eyes and cocked his head to one side, in a fashion that made the words still more impressive. As Sut looked about the group, his gaze was attracted by two figures—a man and a boy. The former was an Irishman—his nationality being evident at the first glance—while the latter seemed about fourteen years of age, with a bright, intelligent face, a clear, rosy, healthy complexion, and a keen eye that was fixed steadily and inquiringly upon the horseman who was giving utterance to such valuable information. The hunter was attracted by both, especially as he saw from their actions that they were friends and companions. There was something in the honest face of the Irishman which won him, while the lad by his side would have carried his way almost anywhere upon the score of his looks alone.

As the entire group were gazing up in the face of the scout, he spoke to them all, although, in reality, his words were now directed more at the two referred to than at the others. When he had completed the words given, there was silence for a moment, and then Mickey O'Rooney, the Irishman, recovered his wits. Stepping forward a couple of paces, he addressed their visitor.

"From the manner of your discourse, I judge that you're acquainted with the American gentleman that you've just referred to as Mr. Lone Wolf?"

"I rather reckon I am," replied Sut, with another of his peculiar grins. "Me and the Wolf have met semi-occasionally for the past ten years, and I carry a few remembrances of his love, that I expect to keep on carrying to my grave."

As he spoke, he laid his finger upon a cicatrized wound upon his cheek, a frightful scar several inches in length, and evidently made by a tomahawk. It ran from the temple to the base of the nose, and was scarcely concealed by the luxuriant grizzled beard that grew almost to his eyes.

"That's only one," said Sut. "Here's another that mebbe you can see."

This time he removed his coon-skin hunting-cap and bending his head down, he parted the hair with his long, horny fingers, so that all saw very distinctly the scar of a wound that must have endangered the life of the recipient.

"I've got half a dozen other scars strung here and there about my body, the most of which was made by that lonely Apache chief that is called Lone Wolf; so I reckon you'll conclude that he and me have some acquaintance. Oh! we was as lovin' as a couple of brothers!"

Mickey O'Rooney lifted his cap, and scratched his red head in a puzzled way, as if he were debating some weighty matter. Suddenly looking up, he asked:

"Was this Mr. Wolf born in these parts?"

"I can't say, precisely, where he first seed the light, but it must have been somewhere round about this part of the world. Why did you ax?"

"I was thinking p'raps he was born in Ireland, and came to this country when he was of tender age. I once knowed a Mr. Fox, whose petaty patch was so close to ours, that the favorite amoosement of me respected parents was flingin' the petaties over into our field by moonlight. His name was Fox, I say, but I never knowed anybody by the name of Wolf."

Lieutenant R. H. Jayne

"He's a screamer," continued Sut Simpson, who seemed to enjoy talking of such a formidable foe. "The Comanches and Apaches sling things loose in these parts, an' the wonder to me is how you ever got this fur without losing your top-knots, for you've had to come right through their country."

"We have had encounters with the red men times without number," said Caleb Barnwell, who was standing erect, with arms folded, looking straight at the hunter. He spoke in a deep, rich, bass voice, recalling the figures of the early Puritans, who were unappalled by the dangers of the ocean and forest, when the question of liberty of conscience was at stake. "We have encountered the red men time and again," he continued, "so that I may conclude that we have become acclimated, as they say, and understand the nature of the American Indian very well."

Sut Simpson shook his head with a displeased expression.

"If you'd understood Injin nature, you'd never come here to settle. You might have gone through the country on your way to some other place, for, when you're on the way, you can keep a lookout for the varmints; but you've undertook to settle down right in the heart of the Apache country, and that's what I call the biggest piece of tom-foolery that was ever knowed."

This kind of talk might have discouraged ordinary people, but Barnwell and his companions had long since become accustomed to it. They had learned to brave ridicule before leaving their homes, and they classed the expressions of the hunters who had called upon them with the utterances of those who failed to "look into the future."

"We were not the dunces to suppose that this was a promised land, in which there were no giants to dispossess," replied

Barnwell, in the same dignified manner. "Our fathers had to fight the Indians, and we are prepared to do the same."

Sut Simpson had no patience with this sort of talk, and he threw up his head with an impatient gesture.

"Did you ever toss a hunk of buffler meat to a hungry hound, and seen how nice he'd catch it in his jaws, and gulp it down without winkin', and then he'd lick his chops, and look up and whine for more. Wal, that's just the fix you folks are in. Lone Wolf and his men will swallow you down without winkin', and then be mad that there ain't somethin' left to squinch thar hunger."

As the hunter uttered this significant warning, he gathered up the reins of his mustang and rode away.

CHAPTER II

A BRIEF CONFERENCE

Sut Simpson was thoroughly impatient and angry. Knowing, as well as he did, the dangerous character of Arizona, New Mexico, Northwestern Texas and Indian Territory, he could not excuse such a foolhardy proceeding as that of a small colony settling in the very heart of that section. The nearest point where they could hope for safety was Fort Severn, fifty miles distant. There was a company of soldiers under command of an experienced United States officer, and they knew well enough to keep within the protection of their stockades, except when making reconnoissances in force.

All those who were acquainted with the veteran scout were accustomed to defer to his judgment, where Indians were concerned, and he was so used to receiving this deference, that when he was contradicted and gainsayed by these new settlers, he lost his patience, and started to leave them in a sort of mild passion.

The place fixed for the location of New Boston was in a gently sloping valley, with the Rio Pecos running on the right. The soil was fertile, as was shown in the abundance of rich, succulent grass which grew about them, while, only a few hundred yards up the river, was a grove of timber, filled in with dense undergrowth and brush—the most favorable location possible for a band of daring red-skins, when preparing to make a raid upon the settlement. The hunter turned the head of his mustang in the direction of this wood, and rode away at a slow walk. He had nearly reached the margin, when some one called to him:

"Hist, there, ye spalpeen! Won't ye howld on a minute?"

Turning his head, he saw the Irishman walking rapidly toward him, after the manner of one who had something important to say. He instantly checked his horse, and waited for him to come up.

"Do you know," struck in Mickey, "that I belaved in Misther Barnwell till we reached Kansas City? There we met people that had been all through this country and that knew all about it, and every one of the spalpeens told us that we'd lose our sculps if we comed on. I didn't consider it likely that all of them folks would talk in that style unless they meant it, and half a dozen of us made up our minds that the best thing we could do was to go back, or stop where we was. We wint to Misther Barnwell and plaided with him, and I was ready to break a shillalah over his head by way of convincin' him of the truth of me remarks, but it was no use. He just grinned and shook his head. The folks all seem to be afeard of him, as though he were St. Patrick or some other sensible gintleman, and so we comed on."

"What made *you* come?" asked Sut, throwing his knee upon the saddle and looking down upon the Irishman. "You could do as you choosed."

"No, I couldn't. I hired out to Mr. Moonson for a year, and there ain't half a year gone yet, and I've got to stick to him till the time is up."

"Whose little boy is that I seed standing by you?"

"That's Mr. Moonson's boy, Fred, one of the foinest, liveliest lads ye ever sot eyes on, and I'm much worried on his account."

"Are his parents with you?"

"Naither of 'em."

The hunter looked surprised, and the Irishman hastened to explain.

"I never knowed his mother—she havin' been dead afore I lift owld Ireland—and his father was taken down with a sort of fever a week ago, when we was t'other side of Fort Aubray. It wasn't anything dangerous at all but it sort of weakened him, so that it was belaved best for him to tarry there awhile until he could regain his strength."

"Why didn't you and the younker stay with him?"

"That's what orter been done," replied the disgusted Irishman. "But as it wasn't, here we are. The owld gintleman, Mr. Moonson, had considerable furniture and goods that went best with the train, and he needed me to look after it. He thought the boy would be safer with the train than with him, bein' that when he comes on, as he hopes to do, in the course of a week, be the same more or less, he will not have more than two or three companions. What I wanted to ax yez," said Mickey, checking his disposition to loquacity, "is whether ye are in dead airnest 'bout saying the copper-colored gentleman will be down here for the purpose of blotting out the metropolis of New Boston?"

"Be here? Of course they will, just as sure as you're a livin' man. And you won't have to wait long, either."

"How long?"

"Inside of a week, mebbe within three days. The last I heard of Lone Wolf, he was down in the direction of the Llano Estaeado, some two or three hundred miles from here, and it won't take him long to come that distance."

"Is he the only Indian chief in this country, that ye talk so much about him?"

"Oh, no! there are plenty of 'em, but Lone Wolf has a special weakness for such parties as this."

"When he does come, what is best for us to do?"

"You'll make the best fight you can, of course, and if you get licked, as I've no doubt you will, and you're well mounted, you must all strike a bee-line for Fort Severn, and never stop till you reach the stockades. You can't miss the road, for you've only got to ride toward the setting sun, as though you meant to dash your animal right through it."

"Where will the spalpeen come from?"

The hunter pointed toward the woods before them.

"That's just the place the varmints would want—they couldn't want any nicer. You may be lookin' at that spot, and they'll crawl right in afore you'r eyes, and lay thar for hours without your seein' 'em. You want to get things fixed, so that you can make a good fight when they do swoop down on you. I guess that long-legged chap that I was talkin' to knows enough for that. You seem to have more sense than any of 'em, and I'll give you a little advice. Let's see, what's your name?"

Lieutenant R. H. Jayne

The Irishman gave it, and the hunter responded by mentioning his own.

"Do you put some one in here to keep watch night and day, and the minute you see the redskins comin' give the signal and run for your friends there. Then if the red-skins foller, you must let 'em have it right and left. If you find you can't hold your own agin 'em, you must make all haste to Fort Severn, as you heard me say a while ago. Aim for the setting sun, and after you've gone fifty miles or so you'll be thar. Good by to you, now; I'm watching the Injin movements in these parts, and, if the signs are bad, and I have the chance, I'll give you notice; but you mustn't depend on me."

The hunter leaned over the saddle, and warmly shook the hand of the Irishman, the two having conceived a strong liking for each other.

Then he wheeled his mustang about, and gave him a word that caused him at once to break into a swift gallop, which quickly carried him up the slope, until he reached the margin of the valley, over which he went at the same rate, and speedily vanished from view.

The Irishman stood gazing at the spot where he had vanished, and then he walked thoughtfully back toward the settlement, where all were as busy as beavers, getting their rude huts and homes in condition for living. In doing this Caleb Barnwell was guided by a desire to be prepared for the Indian visitation, which he knew was likely soon to be made. They had gathered an immense quantity of driftwood along the banks of the Rio Pecos, and the other timber that they needed had already been cut and dragged from the woods, so that about all the material they needed was at hand.

Even with their huts a third or a half finished, they would be in a much better condition to receive the attack of the Apaches than if compelled to place their heavy luggage-wagons in a semi-circle and fight from behind them.

"The gentleman spakes the thruth," muttered Mickey, as he walked along, "and I'm not the one to forgit such a favor, when he took so much pains to tell me. I'll remember and fix a watch in the wood."

CHAPTER III

FRED GOES ON GUARD

Mickey O'Rooney, fully believing the warning of the hunter, could not but feel deeply anxious for the safety of himself and those around him. He was particularly concerned for his young friend, Fred Munson, who had been committed to his charge.

"It's myself that is the only one he has to look after him, and if I doesn't attend to my dooty, there's no telling what may become of it, and be the same towken, I can't say what'll become of him if I *does* attend to the same. Whisht! there."

The last exclamation was uttered to Caleb Barnwell, whom he approached at that moment. The leader stepped aside a few minutes, and they conferred together. The Irishman impressed upon the leader the warning he had received from the hunter, and Barnwell admitted that there might be grounds for the fear, but he added that he was doing all he could to guard against it. At Mickey's suggestion, he sent two of his most trustworthy men to the woods to keep watch, while a third was stationed on some elevated ground beyond, where he commanded an extensive view of the surrounding prairie. As this was to be a permanent arrangement, it would seem that he had taken all reasonable precautions. Not a suspicious sign was seen through the day.

When night came, the two men were called in, and Mickey O'Rooney, Fred Munson, and a man named Thompson went on duty. As two was the regular number at night, it will be seen that the boy was an extra.

"We're to come in at one o'clock," he said, in reply to the remonstrance of his friend, "and I'm sure I can keep awake that long. I believe the Indians will be around to-night, and I won't be able to sleep if I go into the wagon."

Mickey had not yet learned how to refuse the boy, and so he took him along.

Thompson was a powerful, stalwart man, who had joined the party in Nebraska, and who was supposed to have considerable knowledge of the frontier and its ways. He had proved himself a good shot, and, on more than one occasion, had displayed such coolness and self-possession in critical moments, that he was counted one of the most valuable men in the entire company.

The sentinels were stationed on the other side of the wood, Mickey at one corner, Thompson at another, with Fred about half way between, something like a hundred yards separating them from each other.

It must be said that, so far as it was possible, Fred Munson was furnished with every advantage that he could require. He had a rifle suited to his size and strength, but it was one of the best ever made, and long-continued and careful practice had made him quite skillful in handling it. Besides this, both he and Mickey were provided each with the fleetest and most intelligent mustang that money could purchase, and when mounted and with a fair field before them, they had little to fear from the pursuit of the Apaches and Comanches.

But it is the Indian's treacherous, cat-like nature that makes him so dangerous, and against his wonderful cunning all the precautions of the white men are frequently in vain.

"Now, Fred," said Mickey, after they had left Thompson, as he was on the point of leaving the boy," I don't feel exactly aisy 'bout laving you here, as me mother used to observe when she wint out from the house, while I remained behind with the vittles. If one of the spalpeens should slip up and find you asleep, he'd never let you wake up."

"You needn't be afraid of my going to sleep," replied Fred, in a voice of self-confidence. "I know what the danger is too well."

With a few more words they separated, and each took his station, the Irishman somewhat consoled by the fact that from where he stood he was able, he believed, to cover the position of the lad.

The moon overhead was gibbous, and there were no clouds in the sky. Thompson's place was such that he was close to the river, which flowed on his right, and he had that stream and the prairie in his front at his command. Mickey O'Rooney, being upon the extreme left, was enabled to range his eye up the valley to the crest of the slope, so that he was confident he could detect any insidious approach from that direction. Down the valley, on the other side of the settlement, were placed a couple of other sentinels, so that New Boston, on that memorable night, was well guarded.

The position of Fred Munson, it will be understood, was apparently the least important, as it was commanded by the other two, but the lad felt as if the lives of the entire company were placed in his hands.

"Talk of my going to sleep," he repeated, as soon as he found himself alone. "I can stand or sit here till daylight, and wink less times than either Thompson or Mickey."

As every boy feels this way a short time before going to sleep, no one who might have overheard Fred's boast would have been over-persuaded thereby. Before him stretched the sloping valley of the Rio Pecos. Glancing to the right, he could just catch the glimmer of the river as it flowed by in the moonlight, the banks being low and not wooded, while looking straight up the valley, his vision was bounded only by darkness itself. Carefully running his eye over the ground, he was confident that the slyest and most stealthy Indian that ever lived could not approach within a hundred feet of him without detection.

"And the minute I'm certain its a red-skin, that minute I'll let him have it," he added, instinctively grasping his rifle. "A boy needn't be as old as I am to learn that it won't do to fool with such dogs as they are."

The grove which was guarded in this manner, it will be understood, was nearly square in shape, reaching from the shore of the Rio Pecos on toward the left until the termination of the valley in that direction had been gained. It had been so plentifully drawn upon for logs and lumber that here and there were spaces from which, several trees having been cut, the moon's rays found unobstructed entrance. One of these oasis, as they may be termed, was directly in the rear of Fred, who noticed it while reconnoitering his position. The open space was some twenty feet square, and was bisected by the trunk of a large cottonwood, which had fallen directly across it.

Lieutenant R. H. Jayne

Being left entirely to himself, the boy now devoted himself to the somewhat dismal task of keeping watch, an occupation that cannot be classed as the most cheerful in which a man may engage. The excitement and apprehension that marked the first two or three hours prevented the time from hanging too heavily upon his hands, but as the night stole along and nothing was heard or seen to cause alarm, the fear grew less and less, until, like a boy, he began to suspect that all these precautions were useless.

For the twentieth time he stood up and listened. The soft, musical murmur of the Rio Pecos was heard, as it flowed by on his right, and now and then the gentlest possible breath of night-wind disturbed the branches overhead; but nothing else caught his notice. To prevent the feeling of utter loneliness from gaining possession of him, Fred occasionally emitted a low, soft, tremulous whistle, which was instantly responded to from the direction of Mickey. It was the old familiar signal which they had used many a time when off on their little hunting expeditions, and either, hearing it, could not mistake its source. But this grew wearisome at last, and he leaned back against a tree, looking out upon the moonlit valley beyond, where nothing as yet had caught his eye that looked in the least suspicious, and where everything still appeared as silent as a graveyard.

"I don't believe there are any Indians within fifty miles," he muttered, impatiently; "and yet we must have three or four men on the look-out till morning. Well, I s'pose it's the only safe thing to do, and I'm bound to stick it out till one o'clock. It must be near midnight now, and if Mickey should come around here, an hour from now, and find me asleep, I never would hear the last of it."

He felt very much like sitting down upon the ground, but he knew if he did that he would be sure to fall asleep, while, as long as he kept his feet, he was sure to retain his senses. When disposed to become too drowsy, a sudden giving away at the knees recalled him so vigorously, that it was a considerable time before the drowsiness crept over him again.

Thus the night advanced, until all at once, Fred aroused himself as if a sharp pin had been thrust in him.

"By George! I heard something then!" he exclaimed, in an excited undertone, looking sharply about him; "but I don't know where it came from."

His impression was that it came from some point directly before him out on the open space; but the most rigid scrutiny failed to reveal the cause. There was the level stretch of grass, unbroken by stone or shrub, but nothing that could be tortured into the remotest resemblance to a human figure.

"It can't be there," he muttered; "or if it was, it don't amount—"

His senses were aroused to the highest pitch, and he was all attention.

Just as the thoughts were running through his head, he caught the slightest possible rustle from some point behind him. He turned his head like lightning, and looked and listened. He could dimly discern the open moonlit space to which reference has already been made; but the intervening trees and undergrowth prevented anything like a satisfactory view.

"There's where it seemed to come from," he said, to himself; "and yet I don't see how an Indian could have got there without our finding it out. Maybe it wasn't anything, after all."

lIe waited and listened awhile longer, but no more. Anxious to learn what it all meant, he began a cautious movement toward the open space, for the purpose of finding out.

CHAPTER IV

FACING LONE WOLF

Fred's few weeks spent in crossing the plains on his way to the valley of the Rio Pecos had taught him much of the ways of the Indians, and he knew that if any of the scamps were in his immediate neighborhood, it would be almost impossible for him to stir from his position by the tree without betraying himself. The lad half suspected that the sound was made by some wild animal that was stealing through the wood, or what was more likely, that it was no more than a falling leaf; but, whatever it was, he was determined to learn if the thing were among the possibilities.

A veteran Comanche, himself, could not have picked his way through the undergrowth any better than did he; and, when at last he stood upon the edge of the open space and looked around, he was morally certain that no other creature was aware of his movement. Nor was he aware of the action of the other party, if there was really such a one, which had been the means of bringing him thither. If some wild animal or wild Indian were lurking in the vicinity, he knew how to remain invisible.

"I'll stay here a little while—"

Lieutenant R. H. Jayne

Fred at that moment was looking at the cottonwood tree, which, it will be remembered, had been felled directly across the opening, when, to his speechless terror, the figure of an Indian warrior suddenly rose upright from behind it, and stood as motionless as a statue. His action indicated that he was not aware that any one was standing so near him. He had probably crept up to the log behind which he crouched, until, believing he was not in danger of being seen, he arose to his feet and assumed the attitude of one who was using his eyes and ears to their utmost extent.

He was of ordinary stature, without any blanket, his long, black hair hanging loosely down upon his shoulders, his scarred and ugly countenance daubed and smeared with different colored paint, his chest bare, and ornamented in the same fashion, a knife at his girdle, and a long, formidable rifle in his hand—such were the noticeable characteristics, to a superficial observer, of Lone Wolf, the Apache chief—for the Indian confronting Fred Munson was really he, and no one else.

The lad suspected the identity of the red-skin, although, having never seen him, it amounted only to a suspicion. No matter who he was, however, he was prepared for him.

The Apache showed his usual cunning. He was evidently attempting to steal upon the sentinels, and, having risen to his feet, he remained motionless and upright, listening for any sign that might betray any motion of the individuals whom he was seeking to slay, as does the assassin at night.

"He must have been after *me*, for he is right behind where I stood," thought the boy, as he grasped his rifle more firmly than ever, resolved to fire upon the wretch the moment he attempted to advance.

Lone Wolf stood but a minute in the position described, when, seemingly, he was satisfied that the way was clear, and, throwing one moccasin on the trunk, he climbed over as silently as a shadow, and stood again holt upright upon the other side. This brought the Indian and boy within ten feet of each other, and still the advantage was all upon the side of the latter, who stood in such deep shadow that he was not only invisible, but his presence was unsuspected.

The Indian was not gazing in the direction of the lad, but seemed to turn his attention more to the left, toward the spot where Mickey O'Rooney, the Irishman, was stationed. In ignoring the proximity of a boy, it cannot be said that he acted unreasonably.

Lone Wolf remained like a carven statue for a few seconds longer, and then began a cautious movement forward. In the moonlight, Fred could observe the motion of the foot, and the gradual advance of the body. He felt that it would not do to defer any longer his intention of obstructing him. If permitted to go on in this manner, he might kill Mickey O'Rooney, and bring down a whole host of red-skins upon the sleeping settlers, cutting them off to a man.

Fred had his rifle to his shoulder, and pointed toward the Indian. Suddenly stepping forward, he placed himself in the moonlight, and, with the muzzle of his piece almost at the breast of the chief, he said:

"Another step forward, and I'll bore you through!"

The lad did not stop to consider whether it was likely that the Indian understood the English tongue; but, as it happened, Lone Wolf could use it almost as if to the manner born; and it would have required no profound linguistic knowledge upon the part of anyone to have comprehended the meaning of the young hero. It was one of those situations in which gesture told the meaning more plainly than mere words could have done. But if ever there was an astonished aborigine, Lone Wolf was the same.

It was not often that such a wily warrior as he was caught napping, but he was completely outwitted on the present occasion. When he saw the muzzle of the rifle pointed straight at his breast, he knew what it meant, even though the weapon was in the hands of a boy. It meant that any attempt on his part to raise his gun or draw his tomahawk or knife, would be met by the discharge of the threatening weapon, and his own passage from time into eternity. So he stared at the lad a moment, and then demanded in good English:

"What does my brother want?"

"I want you to leave, just as quickly as you know how, and never show yourself here again."

Lone Wolf's wigwam is many miles away," supplied the Indian, pointing northward, "and he is on his way there now."

Fred started a little at this terrible chieftain's name; but he held his gun pointed steadily towards him, determined to fire the instant he attempted the least hostile movement, for his own salvation depended upon such a prompt check-mating of his enemy.

An Indian is always ready to make the best of his situation, and Lone Wolf saw that he was fairly caught. Still, he acted cautiously, in the hope of throwing the young hero off his guard, so as to permit him to crush him as suddenly as if by a panther's spring.

"If your wigwam is there, it is time you were home," said Fred. "We are on the lookout for such customers as you, and if any of the others see you they won't let you off so easy as I do. So the best thing is for you to leave."

Lone Wolf made no direct reply to this, except to take a step toward the side of the lad, as if it were involuntary, and intended to further the convenience of conversation; but Fred suspected his purpose, and warned him back.

"Lone Wolf, if you want to carry your life away with you, you will go at once. I don't want to shoot you, but if you come any nearer or wait any longer, I'll fire. I'm tired of holding this gun, and it may go off itself."

The Apache chief made no answer, but, with his eyes fixed upon the lad, took a step backward, as an earnest of his intention of obeying. Reaching the log, he hastily clambered over it and speedily vanished like a phantom in the gloom of the wood beyond, leaving the boy master of the field.

CHAPTER V

THE APACHES ARE COMING

As soon as Lone Wolf was out of sight, young Munson stepped back in the shadow of the wood, and quickly placed himself behind the trunk of a large tree. He had learned the nature of the Indian race too well for him to give this precious specimen any chance to circumvent him. Had he remained standing in the moonlight opening, after the Apache entered the wood, the latter could not have had a better opportunity to pick him off without danger to himself. Had he meditated any such purpose, when he wheeled to fire the shot there would have been no target visible.

The strained ear of the lad could not detect the slightest rustling that might betray the where-abouts of the dreaded chief, and Fred knew better than to expect any such advantage as that which just permitted to pass through his hands. But what would Lone Wolf do? This was the all-important question. Would he sneak off through the wood and out of the valley, and would he be seen and heard no more that night? or would he return to revenge himself for the injury to his pride? Was he alone in the grove, or were there a half dozen brother-demons sulking among the undergrowth, like so many rattlesnakes, except that they did not give any warning before striking their blow? Had any of them visited Mickey or Thompson, and was a general attack about to be made upon the settlement? Such questions as these surged through the mind of Fred, as he stood leaning against the tree, rifle in hand, listening, looking, and thinking.

Suddenly he gave utterance to a low whistle, which he was accustomed to use as a signal in communicating with Mickey. It was almost instantly answered, in a way which indicated that the Irishman was approaching. A minute later the two were together. The lad hastily related his stirring adventure with the great Apache war-chief, and, as may be imagined, Mickey was dumfounded.

"It's meself that hasn't seen or heard the least sign of one of the spalpeens since the set of sun, and they've been about us all the time."

"How was it they got here without being seen?"

"There be plenty ways of doing the same. They've found out that we were watching this pint, and so they slipped round and came the other way."

"Do you think they will attack us to-night?"

"I'm thinkin' they're only making observations, as me uncle observed, when he was cotched in the house of Larry O'Mulligan, and they'll be down on us some time, when everything is ready."

"It seems to me it is a poor time to make observations—in the night."

"The red-skin is like an owl," replied Mickey. "He can see much better at night than he can by day; but there's

Thompson; let us see whether some of the spalpeens haven't made a call upon him in the darkness. Be aisy now, in stepping over the leaves, for an Injin hears with his fingers and toes as well as his ears."

The Hibernian led the way, each advancing with all the caution at his command, and using such stealth and deliberation in their movements that some ten or fifteen minutes were consumed in passing over the intervening space. At last, however, the spot was reached where they had bidden good-bye to their friend, earlier in the evening.

"Here's about the place," said Mickey, looking about him; "but I doesn't observe the gintleman, by the token of which he must have strayed away. Hilloa!"

He repeated the call in a low, cautious voice, but still loud enough to be heard a dozen yards or more from where he stood; but no response came, and, although neither of the two gave any expression to it, yet they were sensible of a growing fear that this absence or silence of their friend had a most serious meaning.

"Yonder he is now," suddenly exclaimed Fred. "He's a great sentinel, too, for he's sound asleep."

The stalwart figure of Thompson was seen seated upon the ground, with his back against a tree, and his chin on his breast, like one sunk in a deep slumber. The sentinel had seated himself on the edge of the grove, where all the trees and undergrowth were behind, and the open space in front of him. At the time of doing so, no doubt his figure was enveloped in the shadow, but since then the moon had climbed so high in the sky that its rays fell upon his entire person, and the instant the two chanced to glance in that direction, they saw him with startling distinctness.

"Begorrah! if that doesn't bate the mischief!" exclaimed Mickey, impatiently, as he looked at his unconscious friend. "I thought he was the gintleman that had traveled, and knew all about these copper-colored spalpeens. S'pose we' all done the same, Lone Wolf and his Apaches would have had all our skulp-locks hanging at their goordles by this time. I say, Thompson, ain't you ashamed of yourself to be wastin' your time in this fashion?"

As he spoke, he stooped down, and seizing the arm of the man, shook it quite hard several times, but without waking him.

"Begorrah, but he acts as if he hadn't a week of sleep since he had emigrated to the West. I say, Thompson, me ould boy, can't ye arouse up and bid us good night?"

While Mickey was speaking in this jocose manner, he had again seized the man, but this time by the shoulder. At the first shake the head of the man fell forward, as if he were a wooden image knocked out of poise.

The singularity of the move struck Mickey, who abruptly ceased his jests, raised the drooping head, and stooped down and peered into it. One quick, searching glance told the terrible truth.

"Be the howly powers, but he's dead!" gasped the horrified Irishman, starting back, and then stooping still lower, and hurriedly examining him.

"What killed him?" asked the terrified Fred, gazing upon the limp figure.

"Lone Wolf, the haythen blackguard. See here," added Mickey, in a stern voice, as he wheeled about and faced his young friend, "you told me you had your gun pinted at that spalpeen; now it's meself that wants to know why in blazes you didn't pull the trigger?"

"He hadn't hurt me, Mickey, and I didn't know that he had been doing anything of this kind. Would you have shot him, in my place?"

The Irishman shook his head. It looked too cowardly to send a man, even though he were an Indian, out of the world without an instant's warning.

"Well, Thompson is done for, that's dead sure, and we'll have to give him a dacent burial. Whisht, there! did ye not hear somethin'?"

Footsteps were heard very distinctly upon the leaves, and the two shrank back in the shadow of the wood and awaited their approach, for they were evidently coming that way. Something in the manner of walking betrayed their identity, and Mickey spoke. The prompt answer showed that they were the two men whose duty it was to relieve Thompson and the Irishman. They came forward at once, and when they learned the truth, were, as a matter of course, terribly shocked. They reported that the sentinels nearer the settlement had detected moving figures during the night skulking about the wood and valley, and the sound of horses' hoofs left no doubt that they were Indians who had gone.

The death of Thompson, of course, was a terrible shock to the new arrivals, but it was one of the incidents of border life, and was accepted as such. The two took their stations unflinchingly, and Mickey and Fred returned to the settlement, the body of the dead sentry being allowed to lie where it was, under guard, until morning.

On the morrow the body was given decent burial, and the building of the houses was pressed with all possible activity, and scouts or sentinels were stationed on all the prominent lookouts.

Barnwell was confident that if no interruption came about within the next two or three days, he could put the defenses in such shape that they could resist the attack of any body of Indians; but an assault on that day or the next would be a most serious affair, the issue of which was extremely doubtful; hence the necessity of pressing everything forward with the utmost dispatch. Fred rendered what assistance he could, but that did not amount to much, and, as he possessed the best eyesight, he took upon himself the duty of sentinel, taking his position near the river, where he remained for something over an hour.

Nothing of an alarming character was seen, and, thinking his standpoint was too depressed to give him the range of observation, he concluded to climb one of the trees. This was quickly done, and when he found himself in one of the topmost branches he was gratified with the result.

On his right hand, he could trace the winding course of the Rio Pecos for several miles, the banks here and there fringed with wood and stunted undergrowth. His attitute was such that he could see over the tops of the trees in his rear, and observe his friends busily at work as so many beavers, while off on the left, stretched on the prairies, with the faint bluish outlines of mountains in the distance. All at once the eye of the boy was arrested by the figure of a horseman in the west. He was coming with the speed of a whirlwind, and heading straight toward the settlement.

Fred, wondering what it could mean, watched him with an intensity of interest that can scarcely be imagined. At first he supposed him to be a fugitive fleeing from the Indians; but none of the latter could be seen on the right, left or in the rear and so he concluded that that explanation would not answer.

The speed soon brought the horseman within hail. As he neared the Rio Pecos Valley, he rose in his stirrups, and swung his hat in an excited manner. At that moment Fred recognized him as Sut Simpson, the scout, whose voice rang out as startling and clear as that of a stentor.

"The Apaches are coming! The Apaches are coming! Lone Wolf will be down on yer quicker'n lightnin'!"

CHAPTER VI

THE APACHE ATTACK

"The Apaches are coming! The Apaches are coming!" shouted Sut Simpson, as his mustang thundered up to the edge of the valley, while his clear, powerful voice rang out like a bugle.

The words were startling enough, and the sudden dropping of a dozen bombshells among the unfinished dwellings of New Boston could not have created greater consternation, emphasized as they were by the towering form of the hunter and steed, who looked as if they had been fired from the throat of some immense Columbiad, and had not as yet recovered from their bewilderment. There was some system, however, in the movements of the pioneers, for there was ever present in their thoughts the very danger which had now come upon them so suddenly.

In the structure which was nearest completion were placed the dozen women and children, while the other houses that were in a condition to afford the means of defense were taken possession of by the men, gun in hand, ready to defend themselves to the last. Fortunately enough, the horses happened to be corraled within the inclosure, so that, unless the defense should utterly fail, there was little danger of their being stampeded by the Indians.

While these hurried preparations were going on, the hunter remained seated upon his mustang, looking down upon the pioneers with a gathering calmness, as though he were a general watching the evolutions of his army. Now and then he anxiously gazed off over the prairie, his manner showing that he was mentally comparing the speed of the approaching Apaches with that of the labors of his friends.

To Fred Munson, perched in the top of the lofty tree, the whole scene seemed like a hurrying panorama of a dream. He never once thought of his own personal danger, in the intensity of his interest in what was going on before his eyes.

The hunter had scarcely checked his mustang when the lad saw the Apaches appear upon a ridge some distance behind. It was less than two miles away, and they all dashed over at the place where the *avant courier* had come at his break-neck pace; and as soon as they were all over, and stretching away in the direction of the settlement, Fred had some chance of estimating their number.

"There must be a thousand of them," he muttered, in a terrified voice." They will murder us all—none can get away."

His imagination, however, intensified matters. The Apaches numbered several hundred, and, armed to the teeth as they were, brave, daring, and mounted upon the best of horses, they were as formidable a party as if they were composed of so many white desperadoes of the border. A month before they would have walked over this party of pioneers; but there is no teacher like experience, and in the long journey across the plains, marked by innumerable skirmishes with the red-skins, the settlers had acquired a coolness and steadiness under fire which was invaluable in such emergencies as this.

Sut Simpson still maintained his position, glancing from the settlement below him to the approaching Apaches, with that quick, nervous motion which showed only too plainly that he felt a crisis was at hand, and he could delay only a few moments longer.

It was a thrilling sight, the hurried preparations of the pioneers, and the swift approach of their assailants. The latter came in no regular order, but swept along like so many Centaurs, at first well together, but, as they approached the valley, gradually separating and spreading out, like a slowly opening fan, until the crescent was several hundred yards in breadth, and it looked as if they intended to surround the settlement.

Such being their apparent purpose, the hunter speedily saw that it would not do to stay another second. He had come to warn the whites of their danger, and now that it had burst upon them, be emphasized his good intentions by dashing down the valley, and, leaping from the back of his mustang, took his place among a dozen defenders who were gathered in the building with the women and children.

His horse was covered with foam and sweat, for his master had ridden like Paul Revere, and he needed the rest that was now given him. He possessed extraordinary intelligence, and Sut knew that he could be thoroughly depended upon in case matters got mixed, and a stampede was attempted by the assailants.

There was no dilly-dallying. The most serious kind of business impended, and all were forced to prepare for it. In a twinkling, as it seemed, the hurry, bustle, and confusion suddenly ceased. Everything settled down into quiet, and the

Lieutenant R. H. Jayne

defenders, with their loaded rifles, calmly awaited the assault that was soon to be made.

As the Apaches neared the valley, they gradually slackened their speed, but all reached the margin, from which they could look down upon the pioneers, with their steeds upon a gallop, and then, without checking them, branched still further apart, and, speeding down the slope, began the battle forthwith.

In an instant the sharp crack! crack! of rifles was heard from different directions, as the Apaches opened fire upon the whites, who showed an equal readiness in replying. The Indians never allowed their steeds to rest. They were constantly in motion, back and forth, round and round, circling here and there, seemingly at times in inextricable confusion, but with a certain system, as shown in the evolutions of a large party upon a stage, and with the result of never interfering with one another's efficiency.

Some of the Apaches, in the very wantonness of their skillful horsemanship, threw themselves from side to side upon the backs of their steeds, firing under the neck or belly with as much accuracy as if from the saddle. None of them were furnished with the regulation saddle; some had blankets, while the most were mounted bareback. Their skill was little short of the marvelous. Again and again, one of the red-skins would make a lunge over the side of his animal, as though he were going to plunge headlong into the earth; but, catching his toe over the spine of his horse, he would sustain himself apparently by no other means, while he kept up his fusilade. When his horse wheeled, so as to expose the rider to the fire of the whites, the Indian would quickly swing over the other side, where he would continue the same demonstrations.

Thus it was that within five minutes after the Apaches came

down in the valley, the settlement was surrounded by the several hundred, who were circling back and forth, and sending in their shots, whenever the opportunity presented itself.

The wood to which frequent reference has been made, it will be remembered, was situated some distance from the settlement, and, as Fred Munson was perched in a tree upon the other side, many of the gyrating horsemen were frequently shut out from his view by the intervening trees; but enough was constantly in view to keep his excitement up to the highest pitch, and to cause him to forget his own prominence as a target.

As has been already said, the settlers, from behind their intrenchments, were prompt in returning the fire of their assailants. The effect upon persons who had never been brought in collision with Indians would have been to bewilder and terrify them. It is very probable that such was one of the principal objects of the Apaches in making their attack as they did; but it failed utterly in that respect. Carefully avoiding any exposure of themselves, they popped away right and left, the reports of the rifles mingling together, while the warriors, as they tumbled to the ground here and there, showed how effectual the defense of the pioneers was.

The Apaches scarcely expected such a vigorous defense, and, after losing several of their best men, they widened their circle so as to avoid such a close range, and fired more seldom, but with greater care.

New Boston was a peculiarly built, or rather laid out, city. If Caleb Barnwell committed an absurdity in attempting to plant a settlement in the valley of the Rio Pecos, when the entire surrounding country was hostile, he showed some wisdom in the manner in which he conducted matters after the attempt was made. The town was in an irregular circle, with a grassy court in the centre, in which were pitched their horses.

Knowing how indispensable these animals were to men in such circumstances, there could be but little doubt that the Apaches would make a desperate attempt to stampede them, and the whites were therefore on the look-out for such an effort. Not only Sut Simpson, but Barnwell and a number of the principal men, held fire after the first repulse, so as to meet such an essay at the very instant it was attempted.

The Apaches edged away some distance, under the galling fire of the pioneers, until the watchful hunter saw them hurriedly massing on the slope above. He knew the meaning of that the moment he perceived the action.

"Be ready! they're coming for the animals!" he shouted, in a voice so loud that the words were distinctly heard by Fred Munson from his perch in the tree.

All those who held empty rifles hastily reloaded them, and the others, raising the hammers of their weapons, fixed their eyes upon the hideously painted forms, which resembled so many demons about to sweep down upon them. There was barely time for preparation, and in another minute the horde came rushing down the slope, like a mountain torrent, their objective point being the square where the horses were secured. Before they could reach them, however, the settlers poured in their most murderous volleys, bringing many a glaring red-skin to earth, wounding a number of their animals, and creating such a panic that the foremost swerved off to the right and dashed up the valley, followed by the others, while the property of the whites remained uninjured.

The first attack of the Apaches resulted in a repulse, and that, too, when led by Lone Wolf; but the peril was not past. That war-chief had learned the situation fully, and there was no danger of his repeating this blunder. The next time he was sure to succeed.

CHAPTER VII

IN A TREE

All this passed in much less time than has been necessary to describe it. Not until Fred Munson saw that the Apaches were repulsed did he reflect upon the startling fact that there was no one among all the settlers that was placed in as perilous a position as he.

The red-skins were between him and the houses, or fortifications, as they may be considered. He was alone, and although he had no gun in his possession, yet it cannot be supposed that his situation would have been any less dangerous on that account. In the excitement of interest, he had climbed to the highest attainable portion of the tree, where he not only had a good view of the thrilling contest going on under his very eyes, but where the contestants themselves, had they chosen to glance toward him, could have obtained an equally good view of him. Whether or not they had done so remained to be seen.

"My stars! I hope they haven't seen me," muttered the terrified lad, as he began retreating toward the trunk, with the intent of descending to the ground. "If they have, I'm a goner, that's certain."

The Apaches, although defeated, and driven beyond range of the settlers' rifles, did not withdraw altogether. Reaching a point several hundred yards from the houses, they continued moving about on their horses, as though reconnoitering from that distance. The red-skins did not go together, as would have seemed natural under circumstances, but kept up that peculiar restless movement, as though it were impossible for them to settle down into anything like quiet. This action upon their part threw a number of the red horsemen among the woods, where Fred was perched, so that he had every reason for being alarmed.

He was a skillful climber, however, and when he reached the trunk he moved down it, with the nimbleness of a monkey, taking care, however, not to be too rapid or sudden, as the movement might attract notice. Then, too, he had the benefit of a denser vegetable growth, in which he thought it quite possible to conceal himself even from an Indian passing beneath.

"If they haven't noticed me," he reflected, as he crouched upon a limb, and looked and listened, "I've a good chance of keeping out of their sight altogether. It's a pity I hadn't had enough sense to think of all this before."

He continued creeping down the tree, until he was within twenty feet or so of the ground, when he paused, deeming it hardly safe to descend to the solid earth until matters looked a little less threatening. Fred was in a bad predicament, and he was sorely puzzled to decide what was best to do. There could be no doubt that numbers of Indians were in the wood around him, and if he descended to the ground he ran that much more danger of falling into their hands. He could not avoid a strong suspicion that he had been seen, and that his movements had been watched and understood for some time past.

"I shouldn't think those Apaches would consider a boy like me of much account," he muttered; "but if they have a chance to grab me, I s'pose they will. I'm sure I saw Lone Wolf at tht head of the attacking party, and he'll want to pay me up for that big scare I gave him last night."

The afternoon was well advanced, and he finally concluded to stay where he was, provided the red-skins permitted him to do so; so he crawled into the place, where he seemed the best protected by the surrounding vegetation and branches, and, crouching down, he awaited the coming of darkness with an anxiety which can scarcely be described.

It will be understood that he had come down so low in the tree that he could see nothing of his friends on the other side of the wood. He was so near the margin that his view on the right was comparatively unobstructed. Occasionally he caught sight of a horseman in the distance, but the majority of the red-skins were in other directions. Now and then the crack of a rifle broke the stillness, which was so perfect that he distinctly caught the sound of the hoofs of the mustangs, as they whirled and spun hither and thither.

When one is placed in such a position as was Fred, his imagination is sure to be very active, and, time and again, he was sure that he heard the stealthy tread of a moccasin upon the leaves below. All this, however, was not imagination; for he had not been on his perch more than half an hour, when, peering downward through the leaves, he saw the unmis-takable figure of an Indian, gliding along in the stealthy manner peculiar to that race. The heart of the lad throbbed violently, and he grasped the limb more tightly, watching every movement of the red-skin.

"He must be looking for me," was his thought. "He saw me in the tree, and he has now come to kill or take me away."

He was sure that that particular Apache was not Lone Wolf, although he could not be certain that any advantage was to be reaped from that. The chief was not likely to be more devoid of anything like mercy than was the greatest or humblest of his warriors.

The red-skin was on foot, and bore a rifle in his hand. Instead of the fanciful scalp-lock ornamenting his crown, his black, wiry hair straggled down around his shoulders, over which was thrown a dirty army blanket, that had once belonged to the United States government. The hideous paint upon his face was easily seen from the perch of the lad, and the red-skin was as repulsive and dreaded an object as can be imagined.

The scamp was moving along with that stealthy, cat-like tread which is characteristic of all his race; but although directly under the tree when first seen by the lad, he did not look up nor act in any way which would suggest that he suspected the presence of anyone over him. He did not hesitate in his movement, and thus it was that he was scarcely seen when he disappeared in the wood beyond, and the boy was alone.

Fred was now fully satisfied that it would not do to leave the tree so long as a particle of daylight remained. Apaches were too plentiful in those parts.

"I s'pose they'll hang around till night, though I can't see what they're going to make by it," said the boy to himself. "They've tried to clear out Mr. Barnwell and the rest of them, but couldn't begin to do it, and now it won't do them any good to stay here. It'll be pretty risky for me to try and get into the house after dark, but they know I am out here and they will be looking for me. And then Mickey—"

At the mention of the Irishman's name, Fred suddenly stopped with a start, for he was reminded of a fact which had escaped him until that moment. Mickey O'Rooney had gone out on a little scout of his own, some hours before, and he had not yet returned, so that his situation, in one sense, was like his own. But he manifestly had greater advantage, for he was not only fully armed, but was mounted on one of the fleetest mustangs of the West; so that, unless he ran into some trap, he need fear no disturbance from them.

"I only wish I was with him," reflected Fred, "mounted upon Hurricane. I wouldn't mind a little run into some of these Apaches that think they are such wonderful riders."

As has been intimated in another place, young Munson had been furnished with one of the finest of prairie steeds—one whose speed, endurance, and intelligence was extraordinary. There was naturally a great attachment between the two, and Fred would have been off most of the time, skimming over the prairie, had he been allowed to do so, but Hurricane was in the group in the centre of the settlement, with the others, which the Indians had tried so hard to stampede, and he was as difficult to reach, under the circumstances, as were his friends themselves.

CHAPTER VIII

THE SWOOP OF THE APACHE

The afternoon dragged slowly by with Fred crouching, as he was, in the top of the tree and waiting for the time to come when he might descend and make the attempt to rejoin his friends, who could not but be greatly concerned over his absence. At rare intervals, the spiteful crack of a rifle reached his ear as before, and he knew that the white and red men were watching each other, both ready to seize the first opportunity that might offer for obtaining the slightest advantage. The occasional clamping of the hoofs of a galloping horse showed, too, that his dreaded foes were close at hand.

Finally, the sun disappeared, and darkness slowly settled over wood, forest, and prairie. There was the moon, shining as bright and unclouded as on the night before; but the shadow was so dense among the trees that this was of no particular importance, and so soon as night was fairly come the impatient lad was resolved upon making the attempt to reach his friends.

No Apaches had been seen beneath the tree since the departure of the first stealthy visitor, and the hope was quite strong within the lad that in the hurry and swirl of the fight the red-skins had failed to note him in his hiding-place. If such were really the case, it would seem that there was a chance of his passing through the lines without detection.

"Anyhow, I am going to try it," he muttered, with set teeth, as he resumed his cautious descent of the tree.

A moment later he found himself upon the nethermost limb, where he hesitated a few seconds, peering around in the breathless darkness and listening for anything that might betray the location of his enemies. The silence of the tomb seemed to have settled upon the earth, and, hanging by his hands a moment, he let go and dropped lightly to the ground. As he did so, he purposely sank upon his hands and knees, in the belief that he was less liable to be seen in that position than in any other.

The signs continued favorable, and, without any useless waiting, he turned his face in the direction of New Boston and began stealing forward, with the care and caution of a veteran courser of the plains. There was a fluttering hope that, with the coming of night, the red-skins had departed, but he knew better than to rely upon any such chance to reach his friends. If they had really gone, he would have heard something from Sut Simpson.

No more trying ordeal can be imagined than that which Fred endured when he attempted thus to steal his way through the Apache lines to his friends. He crept along upon his hands and knees, for he dared not trust himself in an upright posture, and he studiously avoided all those places through which the rays of the moonlight made their way. There was scarcely a minute in which he did not fancy that he heard the stealthy movement of some one near him, and stopped and lay flat upon his face, remaining thus until hopeful that it was safe to move forward again. And this apprehension was not always imaginary. Two separate times the sound of footsteps were too distinct to be mistaken, and the glimpse obtained of a shadowy figure, as it flitted across a partially moonlit space, was equally conclusive.

Almost an hour had passed, when Fred finally found himself on the edge of the open area which separated the wood from the settlement. Thus far he had evaded all danger and only a comparatively small space remained to be passed over in order to reach the haven of safety.

The boy assumed an upright position, and, standing in the shadow of the wood, debated with himself as to the best means of getting over that narrow but dangerous neck of territory which still interposed. It would be useless to attempt to creep over it, for the moon would be sure to reveal him to the Indians that were lurking near, and it was not likely that he could advance a dozen yards without detection. If it were possible, by drawing himself along on his face, to elude the vigilance of the Apaches, it would be clearly impossible to escape being discerned by his own friends. At such a time, the entire company would be on the look-out for just such insidious advances, and the chances were that he would be taken for a savage and shot by his own friends.

Fred was compelled to do a good deal of thinking, and the conclusion he came to was the next best possible to reach. Clearly, the wiser course was for him to remain where he was for the time being. So long as darkness remained, it was comparatively easy for him to keep concealed, and, while the situation could not have grown any worse, with the passage of the night, the chances were that it would improve, as the way for a safe run across the exposed area would have shown itself in due time. But it was natural that the boy should become impatient, and he easily persuaded himself that his position became more critical each moment.

He decided to make a run straight for the larger building, depending not upon concealment but upon speed. He expected to be fired at, and probably chased by some of the Apaches, but there was a reasonable chance of his escaping both. The distance was short, and he was sure to gain a good start at the beginning; but his main reliance was upon his being recognized by his friends, who would cover his flight. Having decided upon this course, he did not delay its execution a moment, since delay foreboded so much.

Breathing a prayer to heaven to guide him safely, he drew in a deep breath, and, leaping full into the moonlit space, started through his fiery gauntlet.

For a second or two the tomb-like silence continued, and then he heard several hoarse, crow-like calls, which he knew were made by the Apaches. Then came several rifle reports, but he was not injured. It showed, however, that his flight had been discovered. Fred had nothing to do, however, but to run, and he put on the utmost speed to which he could force himself, straining every nerve in the hope of making the log-house, which seemed to recede as he advanced.

Silence succeeded the shots and shouts, and the heart of the young fugitive was throbbing with a wild hope, when a noise caused him to look over his shoulder. To his horror, he perceived an Indian runner on foot, and within a dozen feet, bearing down upon him with the speed of the wind. The poor lad felt as if weighed down by a horrible nightmare, but he bent to his work with the desperation of dispair.

It was useless.

His speed was not one half as great as that of the trained Apache, who bounded forward like a panther, and the next instant griped his horny fingers in the arm of Fred, who uttered a wail, and sank like one dying.

At that moment, the sharp, penetrating crack of a rifle came from the direction of the large building, and the warrior, with an ear-splitting screech, threw up his hands, and fell backward.

"Run, you young beaver! Thar's a chance for you yet!"

The ringing voice of Sut Simpson, aroused the boy, who, finding himself loose from the grasp of the Indian, bounded forward again. But he had scarcely done so, when the tramp of horses' hoofs were heard, and a warrior, more daring than the others, sent his mustang forward with arrowy swiftness, not behind the lad, but directly in front of him, so that he was compelled to turn to one side, in the attempt to dodge him.

Detecting his purpose, a fusilade of rifles was kept up from the houses, but the Apache seemed to escape them all; and, throwing himself on the opposite side of the horse, so as to interpose the body of the latter between himself and his enemies, and, without checking his speed, he reached down, and catching the bewildered lad, dashed up the slope, bearing him away in triumph.

CHAPTER IX

IN LONE WOLF'S CLUTCHES

Poor Fred Munson struggled with the vigor of desperation to escape the clutches of the Indian, who swooped down upon him in the fashion described, but it was in vain; and he scarcely heard the thunder of the horses' hoofs and saw the figure of the rushing mustang, when he was snatched up by the muscular and far-reaching Apache, and borne away amid the shower of bullets, which hurtled as harmlessly about the red rider and his steed as if the two bore charmed lives.

The daring warrior who performed this remarkable feat had no sooner secured the boy than he righted himself on the back of his horse, sitting bolt upright, while, almost at the same instant, the dead run was toned down to a moderate walk. Turning his head, the Apache emitted several tantalizing whoops, intended to irritate the whites into firing.

Although he was within easy rifle-shot, no one essayed to fire, and he knew none would do so. Not even that skillful marksman, Sut Simpson, dared make the trial, for the painted body of the sinewy red-skin was covered by that of the boy, whom he held in front of him, and he who fired at the wretch was much more likely to kill the lad so cunningly held in his arms. Thus it was that the captor made off with his prize, and no one was able to check him, although the hearts of the whites were burning with rage and with the desire to shoot the Apache who had baffled them so utterly.

Fred was still struggling, in the frantic hope of twisting himself loose from the grasp of the redskin, when the latter spoke in his harsh, guttural voice:

"Stop, or I'll kill."

This was said in the best of English, and the boy was astonished, as may well be supposed, at the linguistic accomplishment of the Indian. At first he imagined that it was a white man painted and disguised, but one searching glance not only removed that impression, but revealed the identity of his captor. It was Lone Wolf, whom he had baffled the night before in the wood.

"It's all up with me now," was the thought of Fred, when this intelligence flashed upon him. "He will never forgive me for the way I stopped him last night. How sorry I am that I didn't shoot him when I had such a good chance!"

For one minute he thought of appealing to his mercy, but a brief reflection convinced him that that was worse than useless, and he abandoned the idea as absurd. He was old enough to know that Indians are merciless.

It will be remembered that night was closing in when Fred was captured and a few minutes later, when he turned his head back toward New Boston, he was unable to distinguish a single house.

The mustang bearing captor and prisoner dropped into an easy gallop, passing entirely out of the valley and a short distance over the prairie, where, when he halted, he found himself amid some thirty or forty mounted Apaches. Here a halt was made and the red-skins engaged in a consultation, which, as a matter of course, was conducted in their own language, and, consequently, was unintelligible to the lad, who was as deeply interested as any of them in the proceedings.

The scene was a strange one, and was so firmly impressed upon his memory that he was sure he could not forget it if he lived a hundred years. The Indians he saw now for the first time with their animals perfectly motionless. They were grouped around their chief in an irregular circle, and in the gathering darkness, with their long, coarse, black hair dangling over their shoulders; their low, scarcely perceptible foreheads; broad, misshapen, painted faces and their hideous figures, they formed as unearthly a scene as can be conjured up. Several persisted in talking at the same moment, and they indulged liberally in gesture, so that it was very apparent that something exciting was before the convention.

What it was, Fred could not conjecture satisfactorily to himself. He could not believe that he himself was regarded of sufficient importance to cause any such discussion, and from what he had heard of the war-chief, it did not seem probable that he would allow any such wrangle over a prisoner which he had in his own possession. It surely was over some other matter, probably concerning the action of the Apaches, regarding which he had invited discussion; but whatever it was, Fred could only content himself with looking and listening.

The lad felt that he was as helpless as an infant, and, now that he had been given time to collect his senses, he stopped making any further effort to escape from his captor. Knowing the uncontrollable temper of the Indians, he resolved not to provoke an outburst by any action of his own.

The wonder with him was, that the chief did not kill him the minute he found that he was in his power. They had not shown any desire to make prisoners, when it was so much more easy to rid themselves of their captives by a blow from the tomahawk or the thrust of the knife.

"I suppose they mean to do something dreadful with me," was the thought of Fred, as he shudderingly looked around upon the repulsive group.

There could be but little doubt of that, and he could do nothing but ask heaven to protect him in the terrible danger in which he was placed. At such a time a person's mind is unusually active and a hundred schemes agitated the mind of the young captive—schemes which, when analyzed by the clear light of reason, were about as unsubstantial as the fabric of a dream. Fred felt that if he was not killed immediately there was some chance for him. A few hours, or at least a day or two, would give time for his friends to do something. Mickey O'Rooney, upon returning to the settlement (as he would have to do sooner or later), would not consent to remain there as long as the fate of his young friend was in doubt. And there was Sut Simpson, the hunter, who had taken so much pains to come and warn the settlers of the impending attack. He had witnessed the capture of the lad and was certain to do all he could to rescue him. His long experience in the west, and his numerous encounters with these Indians, had given him a knowledge which would be of great value in such an emergency. Fred recalled too, that he had heard it stated more than once that the Indians frequently took prisoners for the purpose of ransom, and that he might be restored in this manner so soon as communication could be opened between the Apaches and his friends.

It so happened, therefore, as the minutes passed, that something like the renewal of hope came to the heart of the lad, who had reached the conclusion that the subject under discussion did not relate to himself.

This Apache convention did not prolong its session. Lone Wolf seemed to permit his warriors to talk until he became weary, when he said a few words, and the talk ended. During the discussion, numbers had continued to come in, until there were over a hundred gathered together. The moon was shining from a clear sky overhead, and the group gathered on the open prairie, where the members thereof were in readiness to dash in any direction, in case of an attack. With the words of Lone Wolf came the adjournment of the convention. The talk ceased instantly, as if by magic, and the heads of the horses were turned toward the north.

The Indians were about to leave the neighborhood where they had been so roughly used by the whites. A number had already gone, bearing with them the dead and wounded, and the remainder were about to depart—that is, for a time, until their forces could be marshaled into a body that would sweep New Boston from the face of the earth. Such was the decree of Lone Wolf. Was he to permit a party of white men to plant a settlement in the very heart of his country? Was he to allow his hunting grounds to be appropriated in this fashion? Was he to submit quietly to the encroachments of those who had never so much as asked his consent? Not so long as he could summon an army of the best warriors of the Southwest to his command. If his present company had been too small, then he would double and treble it. At all events, the power would be provided to accomplish his purpose.

The horsemen speedily arranged themselves; the head of all turned in a northerly direction. It took some minutes for them to arrange themselves, but they were about ready to receive the command of their chief, when the report of a rifle broke upon the stillness. An Indian, with a spasmodic shriek, threw up his arms and rolled backward, and then from his steed, which snorted and reared, as if it, too, had suffered some injury.

This warrior was directly in the rear of Lone Wolf, and had been so fairly in line with him that there could be no doubt that the bullet had really been intended for the chief. The point from whence it came could not be mistaken.

Over half of the war-party saw the flash of the gun, off to their right, in the direction of the settlement, and those who chanced not to see it were quickly informed of the spot by the appearance of a horse, looking as if he had sprung from the ground itself. No rider was visible; but, of course, he was there, as he had just demonstrated by means of his shot. That there might be no doubt of his identity, he uttered a loud yell, like that with which one Indian defies another, and called out in the Apache tongue:

"Sut Simpson sends the shot for the heart of Lone Wolf, who is a dog and a coward."

This was the favorite taunt of the hunter when he sought to draw out his old enemy. Some of the numerous scars which he received were the direct result of his daring defiance, and he was hopeful that the challenge would accomplish something in the present case. Nor was he disappointed.

CHAPTER X

TWO OLD ENEMIES

Lone Wolf recognized the taunt of his old enemy, and his black eye lit up with a gleam of fire and passion. He would not turn his back upon his white foe, who had just sent a bullet in quest of his heart. He would accept the gage of battle, and end his personal warfare of years. But, like all Indians, the chieftain was the personification of treachery, without a particle of chivalry or manhood, and when he resolved upon his attempt to destroy the frontiersman, it was without any regard for the fairness of the means which he should employ.

He handed the boy to one of the warriors sitting near him, as, of course, he could do nothing when impeded by his presence, although he had proved very convenient some time before, in the way of a shield. Then he said something to a dozen or so of the warriors immediately around him. The main body remained comparatively motionless, while the chief rode out in advance and headed toward his antagonist, his horse upon a slow walk, and moving with great caution.

Sut Simpson was not to be caught napping. No one understood the sneaking character of Lone Wolf better than did he. He had had it back and forth with him too many times not to be able to read the fellow through and through.

While the leader was coming forward in this cautious manner, he saw several other horsemen in motion. Their direction was not the same as their leader. They appeared to be riding further back upon the prairie, as though they had been sent upon some errand to a distant point. But Sut knew what it meant. They meant to steal away until they were out of sight, when they would come around behind him. There were enough to surround him completely and to cut off his escape in any direction.

Sut saw all this and was not surprised thereat. He believed that he was too old a bird to be caught with such chaff. The manner in which he could defeat the purpose of Lone Wolf was by direct fight, or by forcing him into a combat which would anticipate the intention of the Apache. He preferred the latter course, and he made the effort in the common Indian way, by uttering a taunt, still using the Apache tongue.

"Lone Wolf is a coward and a dog! He is afraid of the white hunter! He stays by his warriors, that they may hold his head when his heart grows faint at sight of his pale-face foe."

Anyone who understands the temper of an Indian will see that such a taunt as this was of the most exasperating nature. It rankled deeply in the heart of Lone Wolf, who would have given a dozen of his best warriors for the chance of burying his tomahawk in the skull of his foe; but he was too cunning to be misled by his desire for revenge. He, too, indulged in a little of the taunting business himself; and, as the hunter had honored him by speaking in the Apache language, he "threw himself," so to speak, in English.

"The white hunter is afraid of Lone Wolf. He dreads his scalping-knife. His heart trembles, and he knows not where to hide himself."

"He does not hide from Lone Wolf, for he has hunted days and nights to find him, and when Lone Wolf saw him coming, he ran among his warriors and hid."

"He is not among them now," retorted Lone Wolf; "while he seeks Sut Simpson, the brave hunter moves away."

Such was really the case. Judged from a superficial standpoint, the greatest show of courage was made by the Apache, whose horse was moving forward at a slow, cautious pace, while the mustang of Sut Simpson kept up a continued and equally guarded retreat, so that the distance between the two taunting enemies remained about the same. The hunter had a manifest purpose in this, which was simply to draw his foe far enough away from his support to gain a chance for a sudden dash at him before he could elude him. At the same time he did not forget the dozen horsemen that had stolen out so cautiously from the rear, and he knew that "if it were done, then 'twere well it were done quickly," as Macbeth so aptly puts it.

Sut carefully measured the intervening space with his eye, but Lone Wolf was still too near his reserve. The two men were eying each other like cats, and, although he taunted so loudly, yet no one would have been readier than the Apache to flee if he believed that he was in greater peril than his antagonist.

"Why does not Lone Wolf move faster?" asked Sut, hoping to spur him into doing so.

"Why does not the hunter wait for him?" asked the chief, very appropriately, in return.

The scout thought that if he could draw the savage a few yards further he would have him just where he wanted him. Feeling how precious the passing time was, he galloped his mustang a rod or so and then came to a sudden abrupt halt.

"Here I'll await you, you old copper-skinned hoodlum!" he called out, in unmistakable English.

Lone Wolf did not check his speed; nor, on the other hand, did he hasten it. Let alone, he was sure to reach the proper point in due time; but the trouble was that Sut had no time to spare. The dozen horsemen who were making their circuit must have accomplished considerable of it already, and would soon be closing in around him.

The hunter had been caught in just such predicaments many a time before, and had managed to pull through without material injury; but no brave man who was possessed of ordinary sense would willingly allow himself to be drawn into such a trap. The Apaches were as good riders as he, and a shot that would disable his horse would play mischief with the rider. He wished to avoid any such snarl, and so he dallied and trifled with his adversary in the hope of trolling him along to a point where he could hold him, while the Indian continued his advance like one whose only purpose was to hold his man until the other warriors could close in behind him. The moment speedily came when it would not have been best to wait a second longer.

Wheeling his horse with the suddenness of lightning, Simpson charged at full speed straight at Lone Wolf. The latter was surprised by the movement, but he was not thrown off his guard, nor did he seek to fall back on his reserves. It would be time enough to do that when he should become convinced of its necessity; besides which, he had only to keep the hunter engaged for a brief time in order to give his horsemen the chance to entrap him.

Bearing in mind the deceitful character of the chief, Sut waited until he was within a short distance, when he wheeled and let drive with a couple chambers of his revolver. Lone Wolf went over the side of his mustang so suddenly that the hunter believed he had been killed; but, as he checked himself before reaching the ground, he saw his mistake, and knew that the savage's "reply" would be forthcoming on the instant. Accordingly, Sut followed suit and interposed the body of his mustang like a flash between himself and the red-skin.

He was not a wink too soon. Just as he went over he caught the flash, and heard the report of a pistol. The chief had fired from beneath the neck of his steed, with his revolver—for Lone Wolf carried his revolver, like any other gentleman of the plains.

This was complicating matters so much that the hunter determined to force conclusions without a moment's delay.

There was no use of firing at the Indian as long as he was protected by his horse. He was to cunning to be caught napping. So, without a particle of hesitation, Sut threw the muzzle of his rifle beneath the neck of his steed, and fired straight at the one which was sheltering his adversary.

The shot was fatal, and, with a frenzied leap, the animal stumbled forward upon his neck, and fell dead in his tracks. Nimble Lone Wolf threw himself as quick as a flash from beneath the falling body, and, conscious of his disadvantage, started on a run for the main body of warriors; but Sut, with extraordinary shrewdness, had anticipated this very thing, and, assisted by the intelligence of his animal, he threw himself ahead of him, so as to shut off the flight in that direction.

Everything now went with bewildering swiftness. The Apaches, seeing their chief environed, rode forward to his assistance, while the hunter, revolver in hand, blazed away at him, determined to bring him to earth, now that he had the chance. The activity of Lone Wolf was simply marvelous.

He darted here and there, dodged back and forth, and once or twice actually shot beneath the belly of his adversary's mustang. His antics were confusing, and, although Sut succeeded in wounding him, it seemed utterly impossible to disable him.

The hunter had already discharged his rifle when he slew the horse, and when he emptied his revolver, he was chagrined, furious, and baffled.

"I believe you're the devil himself!" he exclaimed, ceasing his efforts to bring him down, "and I'll let you go this time!"

He turned to flee when he saw that the Apaches were all about him.

CHAPTER XI

HOT QUARTERS

The contest of Simpson with the wonderfully supple and sinewy Apache began and ended in a few seconds. In the most thrilling moments the hunter did not forget his peril from outside barbarians.

The main war-party seeing the desperate straits of their leader, who was liable to be shot down by a ball from the revolver, galloped forward to his assistance, and, almost at the same moment the dozen horsemen that had set,out to head him off put in appearance, all coming from different directions, and converging toward the one point, where the veteran borderer was suddenly transformed from an aggressor into a deeply imperiled fugitive.

It was a time for "business" of the sternest kind, and the grizzled hunter went at it like one who understood what it meant. Rifle and pistol were discharged, and, therefore, useless. The former was slung over his back, and the latter was quickly jammed into his girdle. In a twinkling he had his huge bowie in his right hand, and, shouting to his mustang, he headed out on the prairie, and made a dash for life and freedom.

At such a crisis, everything depends upon the sagacity and intelligence of the horse. It requires something more than speed—it needs a grasp of the "situation," upon the part of the brute, and the guidance of his action which should result therefrom. It was in this respect that Sut Simpson possessed an advantage which can scarcely be appreciated. He made no attempt to guide or control the creature he bestrode; but, bending forward upon his back and clutching his terrible weapon in his hand, he uttered a shout, which the mustang interpreted as an appeal to do his best, and he proceeded to do so without an instant's hesitation.

Still, it was vain to try to dodge through the converging warriors without coming in contact with them. There were too many to permit any such performance, but the wall was not impenetrable. Like an arrow from the bow sped the animal, and, seeing the point toward which he was aiming, the Apaches endeavored to close the gap. The equine fugitive did not swerve in the least, and it looked as if he was plunging to his own destruction.

The scout saw it all, and made no effort to change the direction he was pursuing. He only grasped his bowie the more tightly and compressed his lips. There was an ugly gleam in his sharp gray eye as he braced himself for the conflict.

The nose of the mustang was almost touching the head of the other horses, when he swerved almost at right angles, and, with a tremendous burst of speed, shot through the nearest "opening." This threw all his enemies, by the brilliant manœuvre, in his rear, and left the clear prairie before him as a path in which to complete his flight.

The space seperating Sut from his enemies was too slight for him to reach safety by one plunge. The mustang was scarcely under way, when he was compelled to dodge as abruptly as before, and in a trice he made a third, which was done with cosummate skill, and yet with the unavoidable result of bringing the scout in collision with a swarthy warrior. Sut was expecting it, and, bursting like a thunderbolt upon the howling red-skin, he drove the flashing bowie with such prodigious force that, to repeat an old expression, the first thing the Apache knew, he knew nothing.

At the moment of making the thrust, a painted warrior riding on the opposite side struck a terrific blow with his toma-hawk, but the dextrous flirt of the hunter's head permitted the weapon to whizz by and graze his cheek. The time was to short for him to do any work with the knife in the other hand, quick as was Simpson in his movements; so the tomahawk had scarcely descended upon its harmless mission when he sent out his left hand straight from his shoulder, like the plunge of a piston rod.

It struck the astonished warrior straight in his face with irresistible force and his head went down and his heels up so suddenly that he was knocked completely off his horse—a thing which, it may be safely said, does not occur with an Apache or Comache once in a thousand times, unless it be a bullet that tumbles him to the ground. This opened the way again and the magnificent mustang settled down to the work of life and death.

Sut saw that it was impossible for any of the horsemen to throw themselves across his track, and so he flung himself forward upon his matchless steed and said a few words encouragingly in the hope that it might add a particle to his speed; but that was impossible, as the noble creature was doing his very utmost.

The pursuing Apaches seemed to cling to the hope of

capturing the daring scout, for they thundered away in pursuit, while he as steadily drew away from them. Suddenly came the crack of rifles, but Sut noticed that most of them came from a point in advance, and he raised his head enough to learn what it meant.

The mustang (whether by design or accident cannot be stated) had sped continually in the direction of New Boston, and was dashing down toward that point. The pioneers were on the alert, and the instant they could distinguish pursuers from pursued, they opened on the former, with the result of tumbling several from the backs of their steeds. This so disorganized the hot pursuit that in the flurry of the moment the scout shot in among the group of alarmed horses, sprang from his back, and was soon among his friends, from whom he had been seperated less than half an hour.

Lone Wolf seemed meditating a charge down the valley, and once or twice a formidable number of his warriors were observed gathering upon the slope; but the moment they were discovered such a galling fire was poured in among them that they quickly scampered out of range. The chief, beyond question, was infuriated by the manner in which he had been baffled, and this fury tempted him, perhaps, to a rash deed or two; but he speedily regained his shrewdness and drew his warriors off.

A careful reconnaisance, made an hour later, failed to show a single Apache. The entire body had departed.

The special errand of Sut in venturing out was to effect the recapture of the lad. The chance of success was very desperate, but upon that alone the scout had based his hopes. Had the opportunity been tempting, the Apaches would have done all they could to head off any effort in that direction, but it is often by a sudden dash, when apparently there is no hope, that the most brilliant successes are made. But the issue in the present case had been a complete failure, and Sut chafed greatly under the reflection, for everything connected with it was mortifying to him.

In the first place, he had been completely outwitted from beginning to end by his old enemy, Lone Wolf. That chieftain, whom he detested with the very intensity of hatred, had snatched up the boy under his very nose, and made off with him. The shot that had been fired to bring the war-chief to earth failed in its purpose, and while the hunter was forcing him into a corner he awoke to the fact that he was there himself, and it was only by a hair's breadth that he succeeded in saving his bacon.

"But Sut Simpson don't give up the job just yet," said he, the next morning, in discussing the situation with Barnwell and the leading pioneers. "That younker has got himself in a scrape, through no fault of his own, and onless he gets a lift there's no show for his pullin' out of it."

"Mickey O'Rooney is still absent, and he may be able to help you."

But Sut shook his head. He saw no prospect of any appreciable assistance from that quarter.

"He's a good fellow, and I like him; but he'll have all he can do to take care of himself. When a chap undertakes to go it alone in these parts, he must never wink both eyes at the same time."

"Suppose the Irishman has been killed?" ventured one of the men, who was somewhat shaken up by the events of the night before. "It seems to me that it is very probable."

"You're right," replied Sut, as if he were discussing the question of stock. "Very likely he's gone under. We've all got to come to it sooner or later, and what's the odds if one's a little ahead of the other?"

By this time the speaker was astride his mustang, which was as fresh and eager as though he had not been subjected to the tremendous strain of the night before. The little party of pioneers had come to look upon the scout as indispensable to their safety. His timely warning of the coming of the Apaches had saved them from a frightful massacre, and he now gave them some parting advice, which could not be disregarded.

"You cleaned 'em out this time," said he, as he sat on his mustang, hesitating a few minutes, until several of the sentinels that had been sent out could come in with their reports; "you cleaned them out this time," he repeated, "but don't you think on that account they'll stay away. As I observed to you some time ago, I know something 'bout that varmint, and he'll be back agin, and you kin bet your bottom dollar on it. He'll fetch a pile of the dogs at his back, and he'll clean out this place so complete that a fortnight from now a microscope won't be able to tell where the town of New Boston stood."

"And you urge us to give over the attempt to make a settlement here?" remarked Barnwell, with his old cynical smile.

"For the present I do; I don't ax you to give it up forever, mind, but only to wait some fifty or seventy-five years, till I get a chance to wipe out Lone Wolf, and things become sorter quieted down like. It's better to get out of bed than it is to be kicked out, and you must take your choice."

"But we are here, and why should we not stay?"

"The best reason is 'cause you can't. I don't know as there's any better. It's only fifty miles to Fort Severn, and you can make it easy in two or three days with your teams and baggage. You've traveled the plains long 'nough to under-stand how the thing is done."

At this juncture the three men who had been sent out in different directions on a reconnoissance came in with their report. One of them had climbed the very tree in which Fred Munson had taken refuge. This gave him an extended view of the surrounding country. One of the others had devoted himself to a careful examination of the river, while the third scanned the prairie in another direction. The result in every case was the failure to detect any signs of the Apaches.

Sut Simpson waved his friends a good-by and galloped up the slope, where he took the trail of the Indians and at once set off in quest of his young friend, who was a captive in their hands.

CHAPTER XII

THE YOUNG CAPTIVE

The experience of Fred Munson as a prisoner among the Apaches was one which he was not likely to forget to his dying day. From the back of the steed where he was held a captive he gained an indistinct view of the short, savage struggle between Lone Wolf and Sut Simpson, and more than once he concluded that it was all over with the daring hunter, who had ventured out with the purpose of befriending him. But when the chieftain returned to his warriors alone and without any scalp strung to his girdle, he knew that the fellow had pulled through all right.

Lone Wolf was so exasperated at his treatment that he hovered around for a short time with his entire force, in the hope of balancing accounts with his old enemy. But he soon saw, however, the utter impossibility of that in the present shape of things, and so he summoned all his warriors together and moved off in a northerly direction, his purpose being, as the hunter said, to return with a force which would prove itself invincible.

Fred expected to be handed back to the redoubtable chieftain, who, he supposed, would subject him to the most cruel kind of treatment; but that worthy did not seem desirous of receiving his charge back again and permitted him to remain with his deputy. The lad did not know whether to be pleased by this or not; for his custodian was the most repulsive looking being he had ever seen. He was deeply pitted with smallpox, and the enormous nose which he had once possessed had been splintered by a blow from a tomahawk, so that in no respect at all did it resemble that useful and ornamental organ. There was an enormous breadth, too, between the eyes, or rather temples, the face tapering down to the chin so rapidly that the contour from the front suggested the shape of a wedge.

An Indian almost invariably has good teeth but the mouth of the one in question was filled with snags that projected in every direction; his chin was excessively retreating, and, to add to it all, his countenance was daubed with different colored paint, in such fantastic streakings that an Adonis himself would have appeared hideous. Such was the jailer of Fred, who heard him addressed once or twice by a name which sounded to him as if it were Waukko.

He was, in fact, one of the most famous warriors of the Jiccarilla Apaches, his fame depending as much upon his cruelty as upon his prowess. There are legends in the southwest crediting Lone Wolf with having shown some slight signs of mercy on one or two occasions, but nothing of the kind was ever said of his lieutenant, Waukko, who brained the innocent babe with the same demon-like enjoyment that he silenced the pleadings of old age and blooming womanhood. Fred, as a matter of course, knew nothing of these characteristics; but the appearance of the redskin himself was so repulsive that he could not look at him without a shudder of terror.

The lad sat on the blanket directly in front of Waukko, who held him in place by passing his arm about him. Such was his position when the entire company headed northward, and struck into a sweeping gallop.

It was comparatively early in the evening when the start was made, and the flight was continued without interruption through the night, the horses scarcely ever varying from that same everlasting canter.

The novelty of his situation, and the interest which Fred felt as to what was to be done with him in the end kept him wide awake for a time, and he indulged in all sorts of surmises and conjectures. Without brother or sister, and with only one parent, his father, to whom he was deeply attached, his greatest suffering was the thought of the sorrow that would be his father's when he should come to know the dreadful fate of his only son.

Such were his thoughts when he had no hope of ever seeing him again; but when he reflected that Mickey O'Rooney was still absent from the settlement, and that Sut Simpson was likely to take up the hunt, a strong hope arose within his breast and encouraged him to believe that he might escape from the Apaches.

"Ah, if I only had my handsome Hurricane here!" he murmured, as he recalled the figure of his sinewy and symmetrical steed. "Once on his back and with a clear field before me, all the Indians in the Southwest couldn't catch me. If the hunter would only think to bring him along, it would help a good deal, but I don't suppose he will."

Then his thoughts wandered away to his father, and the tears came to his eyes and the sorrow lurked deep in his heart, nourished by the thought that very likely they would never meet again, and his father's lonely heart would be sorrowful all the rest of his life as he thought of how his only child had been murdered by the Apaches.

The steady sinking and rising of the Indian's horse gradually became monotonous, and, after a time, the boy's nodding head drooped, and Waukko knew, from the pressure against his breast, that his captive was asleep. Could he have had his way, he would have strangled the hfe out of him as he lay thus unconscious, but he was carrying him for Lone Wolf, the chief, and he dare not disobey him.

It is not often that the sleeper rests his head upon the bosom of his enemy, yet such was the case in the present instance. The swaying, rocking motion of the bed of Fred Munson not only lulled him to sleep, but retained him in as sweet and dreamless slumber as though he were resting upon his bed at home, where no thought of the treacherous Indian ever entered his head.

The red-skin sat his steed like a statue. Lone Wolf had entrusted the young captive to his charge, and he would hold him responsible for his safe deliverance, that was all. He might have slept for twenty-four hours, using his scarred and evil chest as a pillow, without protest from him.

When at last Fred opened his eyes, it was several minutes before he recalled his situation. It was just beginning to grow light, and when he saw the figures of horses with their riders he remembered the scene of the night before. When he turned his head and saw the horrid face of Waukko, no doubt then remained of where he was. But he looked upon a far different scene from that upon which he had closed his eyes.

Instead of being upon the broad, sweeping prairie, he was among the mountains. They towered upon every hand, and the war party had halted in a sort of canon or valley, where they seemed shut out from the outer world.

"Where are we?" asked Fred, thinking it polite to open a

conversation with his guardian, with a view of conciliating him; but the red-skin did not seem to be in a mood for conversation, or it may be that he did not possess a very profound knowledge of the English tongue, for he made no reply.

After a time, the lad ventured upon another modest remark, but receiving no attention, he concluded it hardly worth his while to attempt to work any further in that direction, and he gave over the effort.

As soon as the halt was made, Lone Wolf gave a sort of address to his warriors, which Fred believed to be a sort of harangue, intended to incite them to deeds of greater daring than any they had as yet shown. The red-skins became much excited, and answered his appeals with angry shouts, grunts and gestures. No doubt, had he chosen to lead them, they would have rushed back to a second attack upon New Boston, without the addition of another warrior to their number. The oratory of Lone Wolf was not very graceful, but it was very effective. He knew how to appeal to his followers in a way that went directly to their hearts.

CHAPTER XIII

THE ENCAMPMENT

Immediately after the harangue of Lone Wolf a general dismounting of the warriors followed, and the mustangs, which showed admirable training, were left to themselves. The halt had been made where there was grass and water, to which the animals now paid their attention, while their owners prepared for their morning meal.

There was a certain system in all this apparent confusion, and, it being known that a halt would be made at this point, a half dozen of the most skilful hunters of the party had scattered among the mountains in quest of game. By the time several fires were fairly under way, these providers began dropping in, all of them laden with spoils of the chase, which were dressed and boiling over the different camp-fires in an incredibly short time. The Apaches had reduced this thing to a science, and a company of trained soldiers could not have done the thing more expeditiously than did they.

While it was all going on, Fred Munson walked to the brook near at hand, and taking a deep draught from the icy water, he stood somewhat apart from the others, watching the proceedings with a strange interest.

At first he failed to understand one thing. He knew, from what he had seen, that at least a dozen of the Apaches had been killed, and as many wounded, on the night before during the fight. Yet not one of these was visible, with the exception, perhaps, of Lone Wolf, whose scratches from Sut Simpson's bullets were of a superficial nature. The only explanation of the absence of these parties was that they had gone home. Under the charge of a strong escort they had taken another route, and were probably miles away at that moment, and most likely in their own wigwams, receiving the nursing and attention required.

"I wonder whether there is any chance of my getting away?" mused the lad, as he looked searchingly about him. "If a fellow could only get the start, there are plenty of places where he might hide; but there's where the trouble is."

On the right and left of the gorge were precipitous mountains, evidently broken by chasms, ravines, and covered with patches of wood, their elevation being so moderate that no snow was visible upon their tops, while the scene was wild and forbidding in the extreme.

"If I were only up there," sighed Fred, as he looked at the mountain side, "I could crawl into some of the places, where I'm sure they couldn't find any signs of me."

This might all be, provided the lad had an hour or two in which to hunt his hiding place, but the whole difficulty lay in getting that opportunity. It was not to be supposed that the Apaches were so stupid as to give a young captive like him a chance to slip from their hands in broad daylight. They were too shrewd for that and Fred felt that he must wait for some better opportunity than the present.

The meat was prepared in short order, and then the Apaches fell-to like so many wild beasts, using only their fingers and teeth. A large quantity of food was provided, and the redskins were rapidly disposing of it, when the lad saw that no one was likely to offer him any, and he struck in and helped himself.

This morning halt of the war-party lasted about an hour, during which Fred felt that there was little attention being paid him. Considerable earnest talk was indulged in by the warriors, who were apparently discussing some important plans with Lone Wolf, the whole thing resolving itself into a sort of council of war. When they leaped upon the backs of their mustangs, the decision had been made, and preparations made for carrying it out without delay.

The whole party started up the gorge, Fred riding again with the Apache Apollo, Waukko, while Lone Wolf kept himself at the head of the force.

"I thought he would be mad enough to kill me," mused the boy, as he caught sight of the notorious chief, "for the reason that I gave him such a scare night before last. It can't be that he has forgotten it or that he doesn't know who I am; but maybe he is going to do something dreadful to me after he gets me home."

What the real purpose of Lone Wolf was could only be conjectured; but there was reason to believe that he meant to hold his prisoner for a ransom, as the aboriginal scamp was very partial to that kind of business. By carrying the lad back among the mountains, he could hold him against the army of the United States, utterly refusing to yield him up until he should receive his price.

The mustangs galloped along at an easy gait, for a mile or so, when the canon, or gorge, divided in a manner precisely like that which is frequently observed in the highways or streets of a city. Lone Wolf instantly turned the head of his mustang to the left, and, without checking him in the least, continued at a sweeping gallop in that direction, followed by all of his warriors, save three.

These were Waukko and two companions scarcely less repulsive in appearance, who wheeled their steeds to the right. Without any exchange of word or signal, they sped down the ravine and in less than a minute the two parties were lost to sight of each other.

What this meant was a mystery as baffling as the other, but Fred concluded that Lone Wolf had gone in quest of some other party of his warriors, and had sent Waukko and his two companions as an escort to conduct him to some place where he would be beyond all danger of rescue. The shrewd Apache chief, in doing this, only acted with ordinary discretion.

He knew Sut Simpson through and through, and had not a particle of doubt that the hunter was already on their track, and that he would use every exertion to recover the lad. Hence the most important thing to do was to get forward without any loss of time. He had a full night's start of the scout, who could only press his pursuit by daylight, when the trail was visible, and there was no reason why the three men who had the lad in charge should allow the fleetest-footed mustang to catch up with them.

Fred, as may be supposed, was gratified to find his companions so suddenly and greatly reduced in number, for it seemed to him at once that his chances of escape were increased tenfold. It simplified matters. It did not occur to him that three vigilant Indians were as effective as three hundred, and that in a certain sense his prospect of deliverance was diminished rather than increased. He was a boy and as hopeful as his years.

The day remained sunshiny and pleasant, and the easy canter of the mustangs caused just enough breeze to make the riding delightful. Fred felt an unconquerable aversion to the Apache Waukko, whose horrible face and appearance caused him more than once to half suspect that he was a ghoul or demon. He again made an attempt to open communication with him, but he uttered a sort of grunt that Fred took as a command for silence, and he resolved that he would die before he would repeat the attempt.

The gorge continued its winding course among the mountains, some of the turns being at very sharp angles. The width of the ravine varied from fifty to five hundred feet, the walls on either side showing about the same difference of altitude. At times they were perpendicular, and then again sloped at such a moderate angle that a horse could have galloped up them without difficulty.

The mountainous nature of the country rather increased than diminished, and, looking right and left, in front and rear, the jagged peaks were forever visible, the distances varying, but the number greater and greater. At times it seemed as if the ravine were about to terminate suddenly against the solid wall of the mountain, but, as they rode forward, the open way was there, albeit the angle was sharp, and the little party suffered no interruption of progress until near the close of the day.

The noon halt which Fred expected was not made.

He was hungry and supposed that the Apaches were; but, if so, they manifestly considered it of more importance to get forward than to satisfy that hunger. Once or twice they permitted their horses to drink from the water when it was reached, but these momentary halts were all that were made.

It was near the middle of the afternoon, when Waukko, who was the leader of the little group, suddenly showed great excitement, which speedily communicated itself to his companions. All three of these scamps were sullen and reticent, frequently riding for hours at a time without exchanging a word, so that this excitement meant something. The three halted simultaneously, and talked loudly and excitedly, so that Fred suspected that some cause for a quarrel had abruptly sprung upon them.

"I wonder if they're wrangling about *me*?" was the thought that came to the lad, who immediately recalled the fate of Miss MacCrea during the Revolution, when the two Indians conducting her to Fort Edward settled a quarrel over her by sinking a tomahawk in her brain.

If the present excitement could be quelled only by such a remedy, he preferred that it should go on. Otherwise, if there was a prospect of their settling it by falling upon each other, he was in hope of seeing it intensified. It looked as if a deadly fight were impending, when he was tossed to the ground, and the three Apaches instantly dropped to the earth and faced each other.

CHAPTER XIV

THE STRANGE CAMP

The Apaches, however, were not quarreling. They were engaged in a dispute, or rather argument, which concerned them all, and about which it was all-important that no blunder should be made.

Fred Munson, the instant he found himself upon the ground, moved timidly back, so as to be out of the way when the expected clash of arms would come, and he watched the three men with an intensity of interest which can scarcely be imagined. He now noticed, for the first time, that as the disputants talked, they all three pointed and looked, at intervals, up the mountain, showing that the all-absorbing topic was located there.

Following the direction indicated, the boy noticed the smoke of a camp-fire rising from the side of the mountain, about a quarter of a mile in advance. It could be seen plainly and distinctly, although the fire itself from which the smoke came was imperceptible. It was evident, therefore, that the discovery of this camp-fire had produced the excitement among the Apaches.

And why should such be the case?

The fact of it was, that the three Apaches were upon territory which could by no means be considered the exclusive tramping-ground of their tribe. Immediately to the eastward roamed the Kiowas and Comanches, and it was no more than natural that their warriors should come into occasional collision, especially when none of them were disposed to recognize any of the presumed rights of the other.

The dispute, therefore, was regarding the campfire, which had suddenly appeared to plague them. Did it belong to their friends or enemies ?

Lone Wolf, in sending his three warriors homeward with the captive, dispatched them by a round-about method through the mountains, for the reason that it would be more difficult to trail them. The advantage which they had gained in the start, he was confident, placed it out of the power of Sut Simpson, or any of his friends, to do them injury. But here, while carrying out the directions of their chief, they found themselves confronted by an unexpected danger.

If the Kiowas or Comanches, as the case might be, discerned the little company, they would not fail to observe that they had a prize in their possession, and they very probably would show a disposition to interfere. The wrangle was as to whether it was best to go directly ahead upon the route they were pursuing, trusting not only to the possibility that the strangers there were friends, but to the prospect of their getting by without detection, or whether they should go to the trouble of a flank movement.

Waukko was inclined to go directly ahead, while the others were opposed, and, as is frequently the case with such people, the dispute was excited and hot for awhile; but the hideous Apache triumphed by virtue of his official position. Lone Wolf had placed the lad in his charge, and he was bent upon managing the business in his own fashion.

It was agreed, therefore, that they should continue on up the ravine, as this offered so much the better chance for their mustangs to make good progress. Waukko took the lead, his horse walking at a steady gait, while he scrutinized the camp-fire as closely and searchingly as if his life depended on the result.

The flame seemed to have been started directly behind a mass of rocks, large and compact enough to shelter a dozen men, if they wished to conceal themselves. The smoke showed that it was burning so vigorously that fuel must have been placed upon it but a short time before. It would seem that, if set going by hostile hands, the owners were short-sighted in thus exposing their location; but the mischief of such a thing is that the smoke of a camp-fire in an Indian country may have one or more of a dozen dangerous meanings.

In the West and Southwest the Indians have a system of telegraphy, conducted entirely by means of signal fires from mountain top to mountain top. Treaties signed in Washington in one day have been known hundreds of miles away at night, by the redskins chiefly concerned, who had no means of gaining the news except by some system of telegraphy, understood only by themselves. The most cunning and effective war movements, where the success depends upon the cooperation of widely separated parties, have been managed and conducted by the smoke curling upward from hills and mountain peaks. Still further, a camp-fire is frequently used as a way of confusing an approaching enemy, for by what means could the latter judge whether the parties who had kindled it were in the immediate neighborhood?

Was there not, in this instance, one stealthy Kiowa carefully keeping up the blaze, while his companions had stolen around and across the chasm, where they were ambushed and awaiting the coming of their victims? Were not the sly dogs successful in hiding their positions by the very means which would generally be supposed to betray it ?

At any rate, Waukko was not yet abreast of the dangerous point when he again checked his mustang, and the three Apaches consulted in a low voice and with every appearance of suppressed excitement. There was something in the wind which made all three feel anything but comfortable.

The consultation was brief and decisive. Waukko and one of his warriors dismounted, leaving Fred and his guardian upon the remaining horse. Waukko moved off to the right, as though he meant to reconnoiter the camp-fire, while the other savage stole off to the left. Very evidently there was something which needed looking after, and it may have been that Waukko was in quest of information for his leader, Lone Wolf.

Be that as it may, before Fred Munson fairly suspected it he found himself alone with another mounted Apache, both the others having vanished as effectually as if the ground had opened and swallowed them up.

"Now is my chance, if I could only get an opening," was the truthful conclusion of the lad, whose heart suddenly beat with an awakened hope. "If I can manage to get this old fellow off, or if I could steal a little march on him, so as to gain a chance, I could escape. Anyhow, I'm going to try it," he added, and his boyish heart was fired with a renewed determination to make a desperate leap for liberty.

One Apache, however, if he attended to his business, could

guard him as effectually as a dozen, and it all depended upon the disposition this warrior should manifest. Just now his great and all absorbing interest was in the efforts of his comrades to detect the meaning of the signal fire.

Fred sat behind him upon the horse, and he stealthily looked to the right and left, in the hope of detecting some place which offered an opportunity for concealment, for he felt that there would be but the single chance offered him. If he should fail in that, the savages would guard him too closely to permit a second effort.

The ravine at this place was about a hundred feet in width. The sides sloped abruptly downward, growing nearly perpendicular further ahead, so that the Apaches, if caught in any trap at all, would be caught in the worst possible manner. Hence the extreme caution they displayed before committing themselves.

There were rocks and stones on the right and left, and here and there some stunted vegetation. A few minutes start would give any one a chance to hide, but just there was the whole difficulty. How was the start to be obtained? It seemed, at this juncture, as if the fates were unusually propitious. Everything conspired to invite the attempt which the boy was so anxious to make.

Waukko and his companion had not been gone more than ten minutes when one of them signaled to the Indian left behind. It came in the shape of a soft low whistle, which could easily be mistaken for the call of a bird. The horseman started and turned his head sidewise to listen the instant it fell upon his ear, and this caused Fred to notice it. The Indian held his head a moment in the attitude of deep attention, and then he replied in precisely the same manner without turning his head. A full minute passed. Then a second call was heard, emitted in precisely the same manner as before. This was the one which did the business.

The trained ear of the veteran scout could have detected no difference that had been made, but there was, for all that, and a very wide one, so far as meaning was concerned. The redskin had no sooner caught it than he dismounted and moved carefully forward, his mustang quietly following him, bearing the lad upon his back.

The warrior glanced backward only once, to satisfy himself that his steed was there, and understood what was required of it. In the meantime, the heart of Fred was throbbing painfully with hope. He felt as if Providence was interfering directly in his behalf.

"Now is my time," he added, a moment later.

CHAPTER XV

A LEAP FOR LIBERTY

It seemed that nothing could be more favorable for the attempt to escape. There was Fred seated upon the back of a mustang. His copper colored captors were some distance away at the side of the ravine, while the only Indian in sight was a dozen feet ahead with his back toward him. True, there was the risk of being shot, but he felt that he did not deserve safety unless he was willing to run that or any risk.

There was a loose rein hanging on the neck of the mustang. Fred gently pulled it and the beast stopped. He was walking so quietly that his hoofs made scarcely any sound in falling upon the flinty surface, and the Indian, from some cause or other, failed to notice the cessation of sound until the distance between them had about doubled.

At that instant, the redskin turned his head as quick as lightning. Fred, who had been washing for that identical movement, whirled the steed about and started him back in the ravine at full gallop, the brute responding gallantly to the sudden demand made upon him.

The fugitive was expecting a shot from the rifle in the hand of the Apache, and he threw himself forward upon the horse, so as to make the target as difficult to hit as possible. But the Indian did not fire, not only on account of the risk to his favorite mustang, but because it would have been certain to disarrange the reconnoissance upon which Waukko and his companions were engaged.

But the red-skin did not stand in stupid helplessness. A glance told him everything, and, running with extraordinary swiftness to the nearest mustang, he vaulted upon his back and started in pursuit, putting his animal upon the jump from the first. The few seconds' unavoidable delay gave the young fugitive something like a hundred yards start, an advantage which he used every effort to increase, and which, for a brief spell, he succeeded in doing.

Fred's object was to avoid a regular chase, for he dreaded that in such case the superior knowledge of the country possessed by the Indian would enable him to outwit him at every turn. Night was close at hand, and, if he could dodge the red-skin until darkness, the lad was confident of escaping him altogether.

For a short distance, the ravine continued in almost a straight line, and then it turned at a sharp angle. Without attempting to guide the mustang in the least, Fred kept himself thrown forward, with his arms about his neck, while he hammered his sides with his heels, spoke sharply to him, and did everything he could to urge him to the highest possible rate of speed. The animal whirled about the corner, and, with his neck extended, went down the ravine with almost incredible swiftness—a speed which was steadily drawing him away from his pursuer, and which would have carried him beyond his reach in a brief time, but for a singular and altogether unexpected check.

The pursuing red-skin saw his charge quietly slipping from

his grasp, and he must have viewed the wonderful speed of his favorite mustang, under the circumstances, with mixed emotions. At any rate, it took him but a short time to see that in a stern chase he had no chance of coming up with his own animal, and so he commanded him to halt. This was done by a peculiar, tremulous whooping sound, which he had used scores of times to summon his animal to him, and which had never failed. Nor did it fail now.

Fred was careering along at this amazing speed, congratulating himself meanwhile upon his cleverness, when the brute checked himself so suddenly that the rider narrowly escaped being pitched over his head. He jerked the bit, and pounded his heels against his ribs, but it was of no avail. The horse had pricked up his ears, neighed, and was looking back, with very much the appearance of an animal that was in a mental muddle.

The Indian saw it, and repeated the signal. Thereupon the mustang wheeled and started backward at a gallop, directly toward his master.

"If that's your idea, I'm not going with you!" gasped the lad, who slipped off his back, as nimbly as a monkey, and made a dash for the side of the ravine, without any clear idea of where he was going.

It seemed that there was no possible escape for the lad, for the Indian was but a short distance behind him, and was twice as fleet of foot as he; but one of those fortunate interferences which seem to be in their nature like special Providences occurred at this juncture.

The flight and pursuit of Fred Munson took place at a critical period in the affairs of all parties and so mixed up the business that it waa thrown entirely out of gear and almost into inextricable confusion. It seemed that there wea a party of Kiowas in hiding, and awaiting the chance to open fire upon the approaching Apaches. The sly scamps saw every movement of the warriors, and it looked as if the flies were about walking into their trap when the unexpected by-play occurred.

There must have been all of half a dozen Kiowas, enough to extinguish the Apaches, and when Fred Munson started in his flight, two of the Indians hurried down the ravine for the purpose of taking a hand in the business. They unavoidably fell behind in such a trial of speed, but when they saw the Apache about to reach out his hand to grasp the fugitive, two shots were fired almost simultaneously at him.

They were intended to kill, too, for the Kiowas, who were actuated by no love for the despairing white boy, felt that they could afford to give him this temporary respite. They were certain of their own ability to step in and pluck the prize at the very moment it might seem to be beyond their reach. Rather curiously, however, neither of the shots did what was intended. One of them missed the Apache altogether, and the other only slightly wounded him.

As it was, however, the pursuing warrior was dumbfounded, and he stopped as suddenly as if smitten by a bolt from heaven. Leaving his mustang to look out for himself, he darted to the opposite side of the ravine from that taken by the lad, for the purpose of securing cover before a second volley could be fired.

Fred heard the report of the rifle-shots, and sup posed that he was the target and that they had been fired by Waukko and his companion. Instead of stopping to ascertain, he continued his flight with all the desperation of combined hope and despair.

A few seconds sufficed to carry him across the ravine, and among the rocks, boulders, and stunted growth. The panting fugitive was rendered almost frantic by the thought that he was about to elude the red-skin after all. As he bounded into cover, he cast a terrified glance backward, to see how close to his heels was his dreaded enemy.

Not an Indian was visible.

But although Fred failed to see anything of his enemies, he could not but believe that they were somewhere in the immediate neighborhood, and he did not relax his efforts in the slightest. Such strenuous efforts speedily exhausted him, and after climbing, clambering, and stumbling forward and upward for some twenty rods or so, he tripped and pitched forward upon his face, where he lay panting, and so weak that he could not rise. He was sure he heard the footsteps of his pursuer but a short distance away, and the most that he could do was to raise his head and glance furtively in the direction. He had not the strength absolutely to rise to his feet and run away.

Again and again he was confident that the Apache was close to him, but still he did not become visible, and all this time Fred was rapidly regaining his strength. In a very short time his rapid breathing subsided, and he felt his old vigor and vitality creeping back into his limbs. He was ready to spring to his feet again, but he did not deem it best. It seemed to him that the warrior had lost sight of him, and was looking about. If the boy, therefore, should rise to his feet, he would be the more likely to be seen, and if he remained where he was he was sure of being found.

He compromised the matter by crawling forward on his hands and knees, listening and looking, and continually pausing to prevent creeping into the arms of his enemies. All this time night was approaching, and with the passage of each minute came a corresponding rise in the hopes of the fugitive. Fred kept moving forward upon his hands and knees, climbing higher and further away from the point of danger.

Everything remained as silent as the tomb.

The Apache that Fred fancied was so close upon him was, in reality, playing hide and seek with the Kiowas, a business which is generally conducted in silence, unless the stillness be broken by the occasional crack of the rifle, or the death-yell of one of the participants. The footsteps which the boy fancied he heard were all in his imagination. In fact, he was alone. No human eye saw him, or took cognizance of his movements. For the present he was left to himself.

There was but One who held him in view and remembrance at this critical juncture. To Him Fred appealed again and again to lead him through the labyrinth of peril, and to permit him to return in safety to his friends.

Still the boy picked his way along as does the frightened animal, and still he failed to see or hear anything of his enemy. Meanwhile the gloom deepened, and with the passage of every moment his heart lightened, until he felt that for the time being, at least, his safety was assured.

Lieutenant R. H. Jayne

CHAPTER XVI

THE RECONNOISSANCE

It was a mystery to young Munson why the shots fired, as he supposed, by the Apaches, should have checked his pursuer, who was so close upon him. Had he known that they came from a couple of hostile Kiowas, and that they were intended for the warrior whose hand was outstretched to grasp him, the matter would not have been so hard to understand. But he saw the night closing in about him, while he remained among the rocks, moving forward in the same stealthy manner, upon his hands and knees, and his strained ear failed to catch the slightest sound that could make him fear that any of his enemies were near at hand.

Of course he looked with all the eyes at his command, but they also stared upon a blank, so far as animated creation was concerned. At last Fred halted, tired out with this species of locomotion.

"I do believe I've given them the slip," he exclaimed, his heart throbbing more than ever with renewed hope. "I don't exactly understand how it was done, but I thank the Lord all the more for it."

He now arose to his feet and reconnoitered his own position.

So far as he could judge, he was fully two hundred yards away from and above the ravine where he had made this successful attempt at escape. The day was so far gone by this time that he could barely discern the open space which led through the mountain. His view on the left was shut off by the angle to which reference has been made, and on the right the gathering obscurity ended the field of vision.

As soon as he was able to locate the gorge, his eyes roamed up and down in quest of those from whom he was fleeing. Not a glimpse could be obtained. It was as if he had penetrated for the first time a solitude never before trodden by the foot of man. Satisfied of this pleasant fact, he then made search for the smoke of the campfire which was the real cause of his escape.

No twinkling point of light revealed its location, but, having decided where it was first seen, he fancied he could detect the faintest outline of a column of vapor rising until, clear of the crest of the mountain behind it, it could be seen outlined against the sky beyond. He more than suspected, however, that it was merely imagination. Leaning back against a boulder, the lad folded his arms and endeavored to take in the situation in its entirety.

"Thank the Lord, that I have a good start," he mused, his heart stirred with deep gratitude at the remarkable manner in which he had eluded the Apaches.

With the knowledge that for the nonce he was clear of his enemies, several other facts impressed themselves upon his mind—facts which were both important and unpleasant. In the first place, he had not eaten a mouthful of food since morning, and he was hungry. He had swallowed enough water to stave off the more uncomfortable sensation of thirst, but water is not worth much to appease the hunger. He felt the need of food very sorely.

In the next place, he could think of no immediate means of getting anything to eat. He had no gun or pistol—nothing more than his simple jack-knife. The prospect of procuring anything substantial with that was not flattering enough to make him feel hopeful.

And again, now that he had freed himself of captivity, how was he to make his way back to New Boston, where friends were awaiting him, with little hope of his return? He had traversed many miles since the preceding night, and had gone through a country that was totally unknown to him. To attempt to retrace his footsteps without the aid of a horse was like attempting that which was impossible.

While in the act of fleeing, he thought not of these. He was unconscious of hunger, and forgot that he was so many miles from home; but now both conditions were forced upon him with anything but a pleasant vividness. But all of Fred's ingenuity was unequal to the task of suggesting a way whereby his want could be supplied. Even had he a gun, there was not much show for anything like game in the darkness of night, and thus, under the most favorable circum-stances, he would be forced to wait until morning.

"I'm pretty tired," he said, as he thought over the matter, "and, maybe, if I get asleep, I can keep it up until morning, and in that way worry through the night. But I tell you, Fred Munson, I would like to have a good square meal just now. There is fruit growing here and there among those mountains, but a chap can't find it at night. Now, if there was only some camp of the hunters, where I could get in and—"

He abruptly paused, as his own words suggested an idea.

It was a camp-fire to which he owed his escape. Why couldn't he use it still further? Was it not likely that the Indians who had kindled it had taken their meals there, and that there might be some remnants of the feast which could be used to satisfy his hunger?

It was not a very pleasant prospect to contemplate. It was like going back into the lion's mouth; nor, indeed, could it be considered a very wise proceeding to return to the very spot from which he had escaped by such a providential interference. But a hungry or thirsty man is not in the best mood to reason, and the incapacity is still more marked in an excessively hungry boy.

The prospect of getting something to eat overshadowed all other questions, and after several attempts to consider the matter fairly, Fred came to the conclusion that he would make the attempt.

To do this it was necessary to go back over the same path he had followed, and to return to the very spot where he had been ready to break his neck, if it would assist him in escaping, but a short time before. But he reasoned that he had the darkness in his favor, that the Indians were not likely to stay in the same place, and that none of them would be looking for his return. This, together with the prospect of securing something to satisfy his hunger, easily decided the question. Within five minutes from the time the thought had entered his head he was carefully picking his way down the mountain-side toward the ravine.

Fred did not forget the precaution necessary in a movement of this kind. He moved as silently as he could, pausing at intervals to look and listen; but the way remained clear, and nothing occurred to excite alarm until he had descended into the gorge itself.

At this precise juncture, he was startled by the sharp crack of a rifle, which seemed to come from a point two or three hundred yards away, directly behind him.

In his terror, his first fear was that the shot had been aimed at him, and he started to retrace his steps—but before he went any distance, he reflected that that could not be and he stood motionless for a few minutes, waiting to see what would follow. All remained as quiet as before, and, after a time, he resumed his cautious movement along the ravine, keeping close to the side, and advancing on tip-toe, like a thief in the night.

The further he got along, the more convinced did he become that he was venturing upon a fool-hardy undertaking; but when he hesitated, his hunger seemed to intensify and speedily impelled him forward again. At the end of a half hour or so, he reached a point in the gorge which he judged to be at the foot of where the camp-fire was, and he began the more difficult and dangerous task of approaching that.

As upon the night before, there was a moon in the sky, but there were also clouds, and the intervening rocks and stunted vegetation made the light treacherous and uncertain. Shadows appeared here and there, which looked like phantoms flitting back and forth, and which caused many a start and stop upon the part of the young scout.

"I wonder where they have gone?" he said to himself fully a score of times, as he picked his way over the broken land. "Those two Apaches must have come back by this time, and I hope they knocked the other one in the head for letting me get away. They must have been looking for me, but I don't think they will hunt in *this* place."

Fred had made his way but a short distance up the side of the mountain, when he became assured that he was upon the right track. Standing upon a lower plane and looking upward, he saw that the column of smoke from the camp-fire was brought in relief against the sky beyond. The vapor was of nearly the same rarity as the natural atmosphere, and was almost stationary—a fact which also proved that the fire from which it arose had not been replenished, as, in such a case, a disturbance would have been produced that would have prevented this stationary feature.

When the lad was within some fifty yards of the camp-fire, he discovered that he was not nearly as hungry as he supposed, and, at the same time, he began to suspect that he had entered upon a very risky undertaking.

"I don't know how I came to do it," he said to himself, as he hesitated. If there's a camp-fire in this part of the world, it must have been kindled by Indians, and it's very likely that some of them are hanging around, so that if I attempt to get too close, I'll tumble right into their hands. I can wait till tomorrow for something to eat, so I guess I'll go back."

But, curiously enough, he had scarcely started to act upon this decision when he was tormented more than ever with hunger, and he turned about with a desperate resolve.

"I won't stop again! I will go!"

As has been already intimated, the camp-fire, which had played such an important part in the events of the afternoon had been started immediately behind a large rock, the evident purpose being to mislead the very ones who were decieved by it. Consequently, the boy could not gain a fair view of it without making a detour to the right or left, or by coming rather suddenly upon it from behind the rock. Just then it was shut out entirely from view.

Lieutenant R. H. Jayne

Fred stole along like a veritable Indian scout, until he was within arms' length of the rock. Then he sank down upon his hands and knees, and, making sure that he was enveloped in shadow, he crept forward, with the utmost possible stealth, until at last he reached a point where he had but to thrust his head forward around the corner, and the camp-fire would be before him.

Here it was natural that he should pause awhile longer, for the very crisis of this perilous task had been reached.

The silence remained as profound as the tomb. Not a rustle, not the slightest sound, even such as would have been made by a sleeping person—surely no one could be there. The camp-fire must be deserted and all his precaution useless.

CHAPTER XVII

FORAGING FOR FOOD

Fred's fear was that if any of the Apaches were near at hand they would hear the beating of his heart—so intense was his excitement and anxiety. But delay seemed only to increase it, and, pressing close to the corner, he removed his cap and stealthily shoved his head forward until he could look along the other side.

At the first glance, he jerked back as if he had caught the flash of a rifle aimed at him, for the sight that he gazed upon was startling enough. Within ten feet of him sat an Indian warrior, his knees gathered up, his back against the arch, and his head bowed as if in slumber.

The lad's first supposition was that the redskin was waiting for him, and had seen his head as it was thrust forward and drawn back again. But, as he listened, there was no sound to betray any movement, and when he recalled the terrifying picture that caught his eye, he remembered that the face of the warrior was not turned toward him, so that it was hardly to be supposed that he could have observed the stealthy movement. By carefully considering the matter and reassuring himself, Fred soon gained sufficient courage to repeat the attempt.

This time, after pushing his head forward enough to see the red-skin, he held it motionless sufficiently long to take in the entire picture.

The first thing which impressed itself upon his mind was the fact that the Indian was not an Apache, or at least, did not belong to the trio which had had him in charge. His dress and make-up were altogether different, and he clearly belonged to another tribe. The truth of it was, he was a Kiowa, and his attitude was that of a sleeping person.

A dirty blanket was gathered about his shoulders, and his head, with its straggling horse-hair covering, drooped so far forward that the line of the face was at right angles with that of the chest. The up-drawn knees were separated enough to permit a long, gleaming rifle to rest between them, the barrel partly supported by the shoulder, with the stock at his feet, while if the aquiline nose, clear cut against the dim fire beyond, had descended three or four inches lower, it would have been shut off from view by the same knees. The blanket was thrown back far enough to reveal the body, legs and moccasins of the warrior, which were those of a man of powerful frame and great activity.

The camp-fire had smoldered as though it had not been replenished for hours. Still it diffused a steady, subdued glow, from the other side of the figure, as if the latter were stamped in ink, and the picture was a striking one in every respect.

After Fred had scrutinized it a few minutes he gathered more courage and took in the surroundings. These were not very extensive, but such as they were, they were of a hopeful nature. Just in front of the sleeping Indian were several objects lying upon the leaves, which he was certain were the bones of some animal, most probably a deer or buffalo.

"And if they are, there's meat upon them," was the consideration of the lad, who smacked his lips in anticipation.

That might be, but how were they to be obtained? That was the all-important question. It was not to be supposed that the most skillful scout in the West could creep up to the feet of a sleeping Kiowa and gather some food without an almost certainty of detection. But for the fact that Fred was so hungry, nothing could have induced him to make the attempt. As it was, he believed that he could succeed. At any rate, he resolved that the attempt should be made.

"Maybe he'll wake up and turn over," reflected the boy, as he fixed his eyes upon the Kiowa and watched him, like a cat waiting for a mouse to come within its reach. "I wonder whether Indians snore," added Fred, a moment later. "I can't hear him breathe, and yet his chest seems to rise and sink, just as regular as anybody's."

Some ten minutes' more waiting brought the boy to the second crisis in his perilous undertaking. With another ejaculated prayer he crept out from the rock, and moved toward the "feast," as he believed it to be.

He knew where the fragments lay, and, heading in that direction, he moved carefully forward, while he kept his eyes fixed upon that dreaded red-skin, who certainly seemed a remiss sentinel when in an enemy's country. Only a few feet interposed, and these were speedily passed over, and Fred stretched out his hand to lay it upon what seemed the greatest prize of his life.

So, indeed, it proved.

The Kiowas, at some time during the day, had cooked some antelope meat by that very campfire, and had scattered the remnants all round. The first thing which Fred grasped was a bone, upon which still remained considerable half-cooked meat. His hunger was so consuming at that moment that, forgetful of the red-skin sitting so near, he began knawing the bone like a famished dog.

Never did food taste sweeter and more delicious!

If the boy's jaws had been a little stronger, he would have crunched up the bone also—but he cleaned it of its nutritious covering so speedily and cleanly that it seemed as if done by some wonderful machinery.

When he found that no more remained, he clawed about in the semi-darkness for more and found it. Indeed, it looked very much as if the Kiowas had left one of their rude meals prepared for some expected visitors.

When fairly under way, Fred did not stop until he had fully sated his appetite, and there proved to be enough to satisfy all his purpose. Then, when he craved no more, he awoke to a keen realization of the extremely perilous position in which he was placed.

"I had better dig out of here," was the thought that came to him, as he glanced furtively at the motionless figure. "He doesn't see me yet, but there is no telling how soon he will."

And now the extraordinary good fortune which had attended the boy up to this time seemed to desert him. He had scarcely begun his return to the cover of the rock, when he felt a sudden desire to sneeze coming over him. He grasped his nose, in the hope of checking it—but it only made matters worse, and the explosion which instantly followed was twice as great as it would have been otherwise.

Poor Fred was in despair!

He felt that it was all over, and he was powerless to move. He was like one overtaken by a dreadful nightmare, when he finds himself unable to escape some appalling evil that is settling down upon him. He turned, with a despairing glance, to the red-skin, expecting to see the glitter of his tomahawk or knife as it descended.

The warrior did not stir! Could Indian sleep so sound?

Surely not, and the boy just then recalled the fate of the sentinel Thompson, a couple of nights before.

"I believe he is dead," he muttered, looking attentively toward him, and feeling a speedy return of his courage.

With a lingering fear and doubt besetting him, he crept around the corner of the rock, taking one of the bones as he did so, and, when in position, he gave it such a toss that it dropped directly upon the head of the unconscious red man.

This was not a very prudent way of learning whether a man was sleeping temporially or eternally, when so much depended upon the decision of the question, for, if he were only taking a nap, he would be certain to resent the taking of any such liberties with his person. The test, however, was effectual. The bone struck his bead, and glanced as though it had fallen against the surface of a rock, and Fred could no longer doubt that the red-skin had been slain while sitting in this very attitude by the fire.

Such was the case. There had been plotting and counter-plotting. While the Kiowas were playing their tricks upon the Apaches, the latter managed to a certain extent to turn the tables. When they branched out upon their reconnoitering expedition, Waukko was engaged in the same business. When he discovered the single sentinel sitting by the fire, he crept up like a phantom behind him, and drove his hunting knife with such swift silence that his victim gave only a spasmodic quiver and start, and was dead.

Waukko placed him in the position he was occupying at the time he first caught sight of him, and then left his companions to learn the truth for themselves, while he crept back to learn that his prisoner had given his captor the slip.

Fred Munson was terrified when he found he was standing by the dead form of his friend Thompson, a couple of nights before, and so, in the present instance, a certain awe came over him, as it naturally does when a person stands in the presence of death. But, for all that, the boy was heartily glad, and he had wisdom enough to improve the splendid opportunity that thus came to him, and for which he had hardly dared to pray.

"I don't see what a dead man can want of a gun," he muttered, as he moved rather timidly toward the figure, "and, therefore, it will not be thieving for me to take it."

There was a little involuntary shuddering when he grasped the barrel and sought to draw the weapon from its resting-place. The inanimate warrior seemed to clutch it, as though unwilling to let it go, and the feeling that he was struggling with a dead man was anything but comfortable. Fred persevered, however, and speedily had the satisfaction of feeling that the rifle was in his possession.

The weapon was heavy for one of his size, but it was a thousand times preferable to nothing.

He stood "hefting" it, as the expression goes, and turning it over in his hand, when he heard the report of a second gun, this time so close that he started, thinking it had been aimed at him.

Such was not the case; but at that moment there came an overpowering conviction that he was doing a most foolhardy thing in remaining s0 conspicuously in view, when the red-skins were liable to return at any moment and wreak their vengeance upon him for the robbery, to say nothing of the death, of their comrade, which might be attributed to him. So he hurriedly and quietly withdrew into the outer darkness.

CHAPTER XVIII

ALONE IN THE RAVINE

Fred Munson felt that he had been extremely fortunate, not only in securing a good, substantial supper, but in getting a rifle. With it he could guard against danger and starvation. In that country, and especially among those mountains, was quite an abundance of game, and he had learned how to aim a gun too well to prevent his throwing any shots away.

By this time the night was well advanced, and he concluded that the wisest thing he could do was to hunt up some place where he could sleep until morning. This did not seem to be difficult in a country so cut up and broken by rocks, and he moved away from the camp-fire with a sense of deep gratitude for the extraordinary good fortune that had followed him from the time Lone Wolf had withdrawn him from the main party.

"Now, if I could only get a horse," he said to himself, "I would be set up in business. I could find the way back to New Boston in a day or two, shooting what game I want, and keeping out of the way of all Indians. I wonder what has become of Sut Simpson? I expected he would be somewhere around here before this. It would be very handy to come across him just now and have him help me home. And there's

Mickey Rooney. He went off on one of the best horses; and if he could pick me up and take me along, it wouldn't need much time for us to get back home. Ah, if I only had Hurricane here," he sighed. "How we would go back through that ravine, leaving behind us the best horses in the country; but there's no use of thinking of that. Hurricane is at home, and so he can't be here, and I must trust to Providence to get back. I have something now that is of more use than a horse. If I miss with one charge, I can—"

He stopped suddenly in amazement, for at that juncture he recalled a piece of great stupidity which he had committed. He had secured the rifle, and yet he had left without one thought of the indispensable ammunition that was required to make the weapon of any use. He did not know whether the gun in his hand was loaded or not, in which latter case it was of no more account than a piece of wood.

"Well, if that don't beat everything," he muttered, at a loss to understand how he could have committed such an oversight. "I never once thought of it till this minute, and now it's too late!"

The reflection of his great need inclined him to return to the camp-fire and incur the risk involved in the effort to repair the blunder that he had committed.

"*That* Indian cannot hurt me, and I don't suppose that any of the others have come back. It won't take me long to get what I want; and I will do it, too."

He was but a short distance from the place, and, having decided upon the proper course, he moved rapidly back upon the path he had just trod, and in a few minutes was beside the rock, which was becoming familiar in a certain sense. Mindful of the danger to which one was always exposed in that section, Fred peered around the rock with the same silence and caution as before. The result was a disappointment. The Kiowa had disappeared.

"Now it can't be that he was only pretending he was asleep all the time," thought the puzzled lad. "And yet, if he wasn't, how was it he managed to get away?"

A few minutes' reflection convinced Fred that it was impossible that there should have been any such thing as he had imagined at first. The more reasonable theory was that some of the Kiowas had returned and taken the body of their comrade away, fearful, perhaps, that some of the Apaches might put in an appearance again and rob him of his scalp. However, whatever the explanation was, Fred saw that his expedition was a failure. There was nothing to be gained by remaining where he was, while there was unmistakable risk of being detected by some of the copper-colored prowlers.

He noticed that the camp-fire bore very much the same appearance as when he last saw it, and the probabilities were that the Kiowas were some distance away at that very time; but the young fugitive had already run enough risk, without incurring any more, and he resolved to spend an hour or two in getting out of the neighborhood altogether.

There was little choice of direction, but it was natural that he should prefer the back-trail, and, clambering down into the ravine again, he turned his face to the southward, directly through the ravine that he had traversed during the day upon the back of Waukko's mustang.

"I can tell when I reach the place where Lone Wolf and his men left us," he said to himself. "That will take me a good while, but when I do find it, the trail will be so much larger and plainer that there will be no trouble about following it, but it will take me several days to do it, and it is going to be hard work. I need all the time possible, so I guess it will be best to keep going all night."

There was not so much amusement in this as he fancied, but he kept it up bravely for some two or three hours, during which he made good headway. The walking was comparatively easy in the ravine, which was one of those openings encountered at intervals among the mountains in the West, and which are known under the name of passes. In many places it would be utterly out of the question for parties to force their way through the chains but for these avenues, which nature has kindly furnished.

The moonlight was just sufficient to make the boy feel uneasy. He could discern objects, although indistinctly, nearly a hundred yards away, and where the character of the gorge was continually shifting to a certain extent there was abundant play for the imagination.

He had been walking but a short time when he abruptly halted, under the impression that he had seen an Indian run across the gorge directly in front of him. This caused a wilder throbbing of his heart, and another examination of his gun, which was loaded, as he had assured himself some time before, and ready at any time to do him one good turn, if no more.

"He wouldn't have skipped over in that style if he had known I was so near," was the reflection of the boy, as he sheltered himself in the shadow of the rocks and looked and listened. "How did he know but what I might have picked him off? What was to hinder me? If he didn't know I was here, why, it ain't likely that he would loaf along the side of the ravine."

By such a course of reasoning, he was not long in convincing himself that the way was open for his advance. He hurried by on tiptoe, and drew a long breath of relief when certain that he had passed the dangerous spot. But he was only a short distance beyond when his hair fairly arose on end, for he became certain that he heard the groan of a man among the boulders over his head.

"I wonder what the matter is there?" he whispered, peering upward in the gloom and shadow. "It may be some white man that the Indians have left for dead, and that still has some life in his body, or it may be an Indian himself who has met with an accident—helloa!"—

Just then it sounded again, and a cold shiver of terror crept over him from head to foot, as he was able to locate the precise point from which it came. The frightful groaning did not stop as suddenly as before, but rose and sank, with a sound like the wail of some suffering human being.

As Fred stood trembling and listening, his shuddering fear collapsed; for the sound which had transfixed him with such dread, he now recognized as the whistling of the wind, which, slight in itself, was still manipulated in some peculiar fashion by a nook in the rocks overhead.

"That does sound odd enough to scare a person," he muttered, as he resumed his walk. "It must be a regular trumpet-blast when the wind is high, for there isn't much now."

The two incidents resulting so harmlessly, Fred was inspired with greater confidence, and advanced at a more rapid walk along the ravine, suffering no check until he had gone fully a mile further. Just then, while striding along with increasing courage, he came to a place where the side of the ravine was perpendicular for two or three hundred feet.

He was close to this, so as to use the protection of the shadow, and was dreaming of no danger, when a rattling of gravel and debris caused him to look up, and he saw an immense mass of rock, that had become loosened in some way, descending straight for his head.

CHAPTER XIX

THE MYSTERIOUS PURSUER

Young Munson made a sudden bound outward, and, just as he did so, a mass of rock weighing fully a dozen tons, fell upon the precise spot where he had stood, missing him so narrowly that the blast of wind, or rather concussion of the air, was plainly felt. The boulder broke into several pieces, its momentum being so terrific that the ground for several feet around was jarred as if by an earthquake.

The lad was overcome for a moment or two, for he realized how narrow his escape was from a terrible and instantaneous death.

"That was a little closer than I ever want to come again," he exclaimed. "It seems to me that a person is always likely to get killed, no matter where he is or what he is doing. I don't suppose that anybody threw that down at me," he continued, in a half-doubting voice, as he stepped a few paces back and again peered into the gloom.

If it had been during the day-time, he might have suspected that some scamp had managed to pry the mass loose, and to send it crashing downward straight for his head. But as the case stood, such a thing could not have taken place.

Fred continued his flight until nearly midnight, by which time his fatigue became so great that he began to hunt a place in which to spend the remainder of the night. He had not yet seen any wild animals, and was hopeful that he would suffer no disturbance from them. The single charge of his rifle was to precious to be thrown away upon any such game as that.

The lad was in the very act of leaving the ravine, when his step was arrested by a sound too distinct to be mistaken. It was not imagination this time, and he paused to identify it. The sound was faint and of the nature of a jarring or murmur. He suspected that it was caused by horses' hoofs, and he listened but a few minutes when he became certain that such was the fact.

"There must be a big lot of them," he thought, as he listened to the sound growing plainer and plainer every minute. "I wonder if Lone Wolf and his men have not done what they started to do and are going round home again?"

Judging from the clamping hoofs, such might have been the case. At all events, there was every reason for believing that a party of horsemen were in the ravine and that they were headed in his direction.

Fred made up his mind to wait where he was until they passed by. He had no fear of being seen, when the opportunity for hiding was all that could be desired, and, lying flat upon his face, he awaited the result.

Nearer and nearer came the tramp, tramp, the noise of hoofs mingling in a dull thud that sounded oddly in the stillness of the night to the watching and listening lad.

"Here they come," he muttered, before he saw them; but the

words were hardly out of his mouth when a shadowy figure came into view, instantly followed by a score of others, all mingling and blending in one indistinguishable mass.

The forms of animals and riders were plainly discernible, but they came in too promiscuous fashion to be counted, and they were gone almost as soon as they were seen. Fred was confident that thirty warriors galloped by him in the stillness of the night.

"I believe it was Lone Wolf and some of his men," he muttered, as he clambered down from his place among the rocks. Having been thoroughly awakened by what he had seen, he determined to walk an hour or more longer, for he felt that the best time for him to journey was during the protecting darkness of night.

"There ain't anybody to make me get up early," he reasoned, "and when I go to sleep I can stick to it as long as I want to. It seems to me that if I walk all I can tonight, and keep at it the most of tomorrow, I ought to be somewhere near the place where we came in among these mountains. Then a day or two's tramping over the back trail will take me pretty nearly to New Boston—that is, if nobody gobbles me up. I've got a rough road before me, but God has guided me thus far, and I'll trust him clean through. I've had some wonderful escapes to tell about—"

He was too wide awake and too much on the alert to forget precisely where he was, or to fail to take in whatever should occur of an alarming nature. That which now startled him and suddenly cut short his musings was the sound of a horse's hoofs, close behind him.

Fred had been duped by his own fears and imaginings so many times that he could not be served so again, and, as he was not apprehending anything of the kind at that moment, there was no possibility of escape from the reality of the sound. He halted and turned his head like lightning, grasping his rifle in his nervous, determined way as he peered back into the gloom, whispering to himself:

"That must be Lone Wolf or some of the warriors coming back to look for me."

This was rather vague theorizing, however. Look and stare as much as he chose, he could detect nothing that resembled man or animal. He shrank to one side and waited several minutes, in the hope that ihe thing would explain itself. But it did not, and, after waiting some time, he resumed his journey along the ravine, keeping close to the shadow on the right side, and using eyes and ears to guard against the insidious approach of any kind of foe.

Sometimes, under such circumstances, when a sound has very nearly or quite died out In the stillness, there seems to come a peculiar eddy or turn of wind, or that which causes the sound, passes for an instant at a point which is so situated as to impel the waves of air directly to the ear of the listener. Fred did not exactly understand how this thing could happen, but he had known of something of the kind, and he was gradually bringing himself to explain the thing in that fashion, when his theory was upset by such a sudden, violent rattling of hoofs, so close behind him, that he leaped to one side, fearful of being trampled upon.

"That's a pretty way to come upon a fellow!" he gasped, whirling about with the purpose of shooting the red-skin for his startling introduction.

But neither rider nor horseman was visible.

The watcher could scarcely believe the evidence of his own senses. It seemed to him that the Apache, as he believed him to be, must have turned abruptly aside, into some opening in the side of the ravine, but he could not remember having seen any place that would admit of such strategy. When he came to reflect upon it, it seemed impossible.

"Well, that beats everything," he said, with a perplexed sigh. "That sounded so close that I expected to be run over before I could get out of the way, and now he's gone."

He waited some minutes, and, hearing and seeing nothing, once more resumed his stealthy way along the gorge, a new, shivering fear gradually creeping over him, as it does over anyone who suspects himself in the presence of the unexplainable and unnatural.

"I wonder whether they have ghosts in this part of the world?" he said to himself. "I used to hear the men talk of such things, but father said there was nothing in them, and so I didn't believe them—but I don't know what father would say or think if he was in my place."

There was the strong counter-belief, also—the conviction that most likely there was a reality about the thing—which kept Fred on the *qui vive*. He was determined, if possible, to prevent a repetition of the startling surprise of a few minutes before. He scrutinized the side of the ravine as he walked along, on the lookout for any opening or crevice which would permit a man and a horse to find shelter. It did not seem possible that any retreat that would shelter them could escape the eyes of the lad.

"I haven't seen any such place yet, so, if the Indian is trying any such trick, he can't do it here without my seeing him, and if I do—Heaven save me!"

He sprang to one side, again pressing himself back against the rock, as though trying to flatten his body there in order to escape the trampling hoofs. At the same time he cocked his rifle, with the purpose of giving the finishing touch to the Apache who had alarmed him once too often in this fashion.

CHAPTER XX

AN UNCOMFORTABLE LODGING

A more astounding surprise than before awaited the lad. His hair almost lifted itself as he found himself staring at vacancy, with no sign of a living person in sight. Whatever had been the cause of this mysterious performance, it was very apparent that the solution rested not with the young fugitive.

"I'm tired of this," he exclaimed, impatiently, after he had waited several minutes, "and it isn't going to be played on me again."

With this, he began clambering up out of the ravine, with the resolve to reach some place where no shadowy horseman could ride over him.

The climbing was difficult at first, but he soon reached a point where the inclination was not so steep, and where he could progress with much more ease and facility. In this way he in time reached the upper level, and, believing himself out of range of his phantom pursuer, had time to look about for some sleeping-place for the night.

He frequently paused and listened, but could not see or hear anything of man or beast, and, confident that no danger was to be apprehended from either, he devoted himself to hunting for some refuge, that he could consider secure against molestation. His first inclination was to seek out a place among the rocks, as he was likely to gain room where he could stretch out at his ease and enjoy a few hours' slumber, but, on reflection, there were several objections to this.

In that part of the world were an abundance of poisonous serpents, and he had a natural dread of disturbing some of them.

"If I can find the right kind of tree, I think that will be the best sort of a place, for nothing could get at me there, and there may be all the limbs I want to make a bed. I guess there's the location now."

He was walking along all the time that he had been thinking and talking, and, at this juncture, he approached a straggling group of trees, which seemed likely to offer the very refuge he was seeking. He made his way toward them with quickened steps.

Fred found himself upon a sort of plateau, broken here and there by rocks, boulders, and irregularities of surface, but in the main easy to be traversed, and he lost no time in making a survey of the grove which had caught his eye. There were some twenty in all, and several of them offered the very shelter. The limbs were no more than six or eight feet above the ground, and the largest trees were fifty feet in height, the branches appearing dense, and capable, apparently, of affording as firm a support as anyone could need while asleep.

"I guess that will do," he concluded, after surveying the largest, which happened to stand on the outer edge of the grove. "If I can get the bed, there ain't any danger of being bothered by snakes and wild animals."

Fred naturally pondered a moment as to the best means of climbing into the tree with his gun. It was full size, and of such weight that he had been considerably wearied in carrying it such a distance, but it contained a precious charge, to be used in some emergency that was likely to arise, and no man was wealthy enough to buy it from him. The way that he decided upon was to leave the gun against the trunk of the tree, and then climb in the way that comes natural to a boy. The barrel of course, would bother him a little, but he could pull through very well, and he immediately set about doing so.

As he expected, the gun got in his way, but he managed it very well, without knocking it down, and in a few minutes had climbed high enough to grasp the first limb with one hand, which was all that he desired, as he could easily draw himself up in that fashion.

Fred had just made his grasp certain, when he heard a peculiar yelp, and a rush of something by him.

Not knowing what it meant, but apprehending some new danger, he drew himself upon the limb with a spasmodic effort, and then turned to see what it meant. To his amazement and terror, he discovered that it was an immense wolf, which had made a snap at and narrowly missed his heels. It had come like a shadow, making no announcement of its presence, and a second or two sooner would have brought the two into collision.

As Fred looked downward the wolf looked upward, and the two glared at each other for a minute or so, as if they meant to stare each other out of countenance. The wolf was unusually large, belonging to what is known as the mountain species, and he seemed capable of leaping up among the limbs without any extra effort; but wolves are not addicted to climbing trees, and the one in question seemed to content himself with looking up and meditating upon the situation. It seemed to the lad that he was saying:

"Well, young man, you're up there out of my reach, but I can afford to wait; you'll have to come down pretty soon."

"If I only had some powder and ball," reflected Fred, "I'd soon wipe you out."

The temptation was very strong to spend the last bullet upon him, but he could not fail to see the absurdity of the thing; besides which, his gun was seated upon the ground, with the muzzle pointed upward at him. He could reach it from his perch on the lowermost limb, but it was hardly safe to attempt it while his enemy was seated there upon his haunches, as if debating whether he should go up or not.

The boy was in terror lest the brute should strike the piece and knock it down, in which case it was likely to be discharged and to be placed altogether beyond his reach. But the dreaded creature sat as motionless as if he were a carved statue in front of some gentleman's residence, his eyes fixed upon his supper, which had escaped him by such a narrow chance. The situation was about as interesting as it could well be, and, in fact, it was rather too interesting for Fred, who was alarmed at the prospect of being besieged by a mountain wolf.

After the lapse of a minute or two, the brute quietly rose from his haunches, trotted a few paces, and then gave utterance to the dismal wail peculiar to his species. It had a baying, howling tone, which made the chills creep over the boy from head to foot. He had heard the barking and howling of wolves when crossing the prairies, but there was deep, thunderous bass to the one which now struck upon his ear such as he had never before heard, and which gave it a significance that was like a voice from the tomb.

The instant the brute left his station, Fred reached down, seized the muzzle of his gun, and drew it up. Then he made his way some twenty feet above, where he could feel secure against any daring leap from his foe. He had scarcely perched himself in this position, when the bay of the wolf was answered from fully a dozen different directions.

He had called to his comrades, and their replies came from every point of the compass—the same rumbling, hoarse, wailing howls that had notified them where a prize awaited them. A minute later, the brute trotted back to his place, where he sat down until the arrival of reinforcements.

"It isn't one wolf, but a hundred, that going to besiege me!" gasped the terrified boy.

He spoke the truth.

CHAPTER XXI

A TERRIBLE NIGHT

The prospect of being besieged all night in a tree by a pack of mountain wolves was not a pleasant one by any means, and Fred, who had climbed up among the branches with the object of securing a few hours' slumber, found little chance of closing his eyes for even a minute.

"It might have been worse," he reflected, as he listened to the dismal howling, "for if they had happened to come down upon me when I was walking along the ravine, I couldn't have gotten into any place like this in time to save me. Wolves don't know how to climb trees, and so long as I stay here I'm all right; but I can't stay here forever."

By-and-by there was a sharp pattering upon the ground, and then the hoarse howling changed to quick, dog-like yelps, such as these animals emit when leaping down upon their prey, and which may be supposed to mean exultation.

Fred came down sufficiently far from his perch to get a glimpse of the ground beneath. He saw nearly a score of huge mountain wolves, bounding hither and thither, and over each other, and back and forth, as though going through some preliminary exercise, so as to prepare themselves for the feast that was soon to be theirs.

"If I was down there," thought the boy, with a shudder, "I suppose I'd last them about two minutes, and then they'd be hungrier than ever. They'll stay there all night, but I wonder if they'll go away in the morning. If they don't, I can't tell what's to become of me."

He watched them awhile with a lingering fear that some of them might manage to get among the branches, but they did not make the attempt. They had sufficient dexterity to leap from the ground up among the lowermost limbs, but had no power of retaining their position, or doing anything after they got there.

Nature had unfitted them for such work, and they did not try it. They seemed to possess tireless activity, and they kept up their leaping and frolicing as though they had nothing else in the world to do.

After watching them until he was tired, Fred carefully climbed up among the branches again, where he secured himself as firmly as was possible. He had lain his rifle across a couple of limbs above his head, and fixed upon a place within a dozen feet or so of the top, as the one offering the best support.

Here two or three limbs were gnarled and twisted in such a way that he could seat himself and arrange his body in such a way that he could have enjoyed a night's slumber with as much refreshment as if stretched out upon a blanket on the ground. But the serenade below was not calculated to soothe his nerves into soft, downy sleep, and he shuddered at the thought of sitting where he was for four or five hours, with the pattering feet below him, varied by a yelp or howl, when he should feel disposed to close his eyes.

"But, then, it can't be helped," he added to himself, endeavoring to look philosophically at the matter. "I ought to be thankful that they didn't catch me before I reached the tree, and so I am; and I would be very thankful, too, if they would go away and leave me alone. I've got a bed here twice as good as I expected to find, and could sleep as well as anywhere else."

Almost any sound long continued becomes monotonous, and thus it was that scarcely a half-hour had passed when, in spite of the dreadful beasts below, his eyes began to grow heavy and his head to droop.

But at this juncture he received a terrible shock. Just as everything was becoming dreamy and unreal, he was startled by a jarring of the tree, as though struck with some heavy object. When it was repeated several times, his senses returned to him, and he raised his head and listened.

"I wonder what that can be?" he said to himself. "Is some one hitting the tree? No, it isn't that."

It seemed not so much a jarring of the trunk as a swaying of the whole tree.

Puzzled and alarmed, Fred drew his legs from their rather cramped position, and picked his way downward among the limbs until he had descended far enough to inform himself.

"Heaven save me! they're in the tree!" he gasped, paralyzed for the moment with terror.

In one sense, such was the case. The frolicsome wolves had varied their amusement by springing upward among the lowermost branches. A brute would make a jump, and, landing upon the limb, sustain himself until one or two of his comrades imitated his performance, when they would all come tumbling to the ground.

Thus, it may be said, they were climbing the tree, but they were scarcely in it when they were out of it again, and Fred had nothing to fear from that source.

In his fright, he hastily clambered back again after his rifle, with the intention of shooting the one that was nearest, but by the time he laid his hand upon the weapon his terror had lessened so much that he concluded to wait until assured that it was necessary. And a few minutes' waiting convinced him that he had nothing to fear from that source. It was only another phase of the hilarious fun they were keeping up for their own amusement.

"I guess I'll try it again," concluded Fred, as he proceeded to stow his arms and legs into position for the nap which he came so near commencing a few minutes before.

He did not consider it within the range of possibility that he could unconsciously displace his limbs during sleep sufficiently to permit him to fall.

He heard the yelping and occasional baying below, the rustling among the limbs, and the undulation caused by the animals leaping upward among the branches; but they ceased to disturb him after a time, and became like the sound of falling water in the ears of the hunter by his camp-fire. It was not long before slumber stole away his senses, and he slept.

A healthful boy generally sleeps well, and is untroubled by dreams, unless he has been indulging in some indiscretion in the way of diet, but the stirring scenes of the last few days were so impressed upon the mind of Fred that they reappeared in his visions of night, as he lived them all over again. He was again standing in the silent wood along the Rio Pecos, with Mickey O'Rooney, watching for the stealthy approach of the Apaches. As time passed, he saw the excited figure of Sut Simpson the scout, as he came thundering over the prairie, with his warning cry of the approach of the red-skins. The rattling fight in front of the young settlement, the repulse of the Apaches, the swoop of Lone Wolf and the lad's capture, the night ride, the encampment among the mountains, his own singular escape, and, finally, his siege by the mountain wolves—all these passed through the mind of the sleeping lad, and finally settled down to a hand-to-hand fight with the leader of the brutes.

Fred fancied that the two had met in the ravine, and, clubbing his gun, he whacked the beast over his head every time he leaped at him. He struck him royal, resounding blows, too, but, somehow or other, they failed to produce any effect. The wolf kept coming and coming again, until, at last, the boy concluded he would wind up the bout by jumping upon, and throwing him down, and then deliberately choking him to death.

He made the jump, and awakening instantly, found he had leaped "out of bed," and was falling downward through the limbs. It all flashed upon the lad with the suddenness of lightning.

He remembered the ravenous wolves, and, with a shuddering horror which cannot be pictured or imagined, felt that he was dropping directly into their fangs. It was the instinct of nature which caused him to throw out his feet and hands in the hope of checking his fall.

By a hair's breadth he succeeded. But it was nearly the lowermost limb which he grasped with his desperate clutch, and hung with his arms dangling within reach of the wolves below.

The famished brutes seemed to be expecting this choice tid-bit to drop into their maws, and their yelps and howls became wilder than ever, and they nearly broke each other's necks in their furious frolicing back and forth.

The moment young Munson succeeded in checking himself, he made a quick effort to draw up his feet and regain his place beyond the reach of the brutes. It was done in a twinkling, but not soon enough to escape one of the creatures, which made a leap and fastened upon his foot.

The lad was just twisting himself over the limb, when he felt one of his shoes seized in the jaws of a wolf. The sudden addition to his weight drew him down again, and almost jerked his hold from the limb, in which event he would have been snapped up and disposed of before he could have made a struggle in the way of resistance. But he held on, and with an unnatural spasm of strength, drew himself and the clogging weight part way up, kicking both feet with the fury of despair.

The wolf held fast to one shoe, while the heel of the other was jammed into his eyes. This, however, would not have dislodged him, had not his own comrades interfered, and defeated the brute by their own eager greediness. Seeing that the first one had fastened to the prize, a half-dozen of them began leaping upward with the purpose of securing a share in the same. In this way they got into each other's way, and all came tumbling to the ground in a heap.

Before they could repeat the performance the terrified lad was a dozen feet beyond their reach, and climbing still higher.

When Fred reached his former perch, he was in doubt whether he should halt or go still higher. His heart was throbbing violently, and he was white and panting from the frightful shock he had received.

"That was awful!" he gasped, as he reflected upon what had taken place. "I don't know what saved me from death! Yes, I do; it was God!" he added, looking up through the leaves to the clear, moonlit sky above him. "He has brought me through a good many dangers, and He will not forsake me."

After such an experience, it was impossible that sleep should return to the eyes of the lad. He resumed his old perch, but only because it was the most comfortable. Had he believed that there was a possibility of slumber, he would have fought it off, but there was not.

"I'll wait here till morning," he said to himself. "It must be close at hand; and then, maybe, they will go away."

He looked longingly for some sign of the breaking of day, but the moonlight, for a long time, was unrelieved by the rose-flush of the morning.

CHAPTER XXII

LOST

Following the escape of their human victim, the wolves had maintained a frightful and most discordant howling, as if angered beyond expression at the style in which they had been baffled of their prey.

The lad sat listening to this, when suddenly it ceased. Silence from each beast came as completely and simultaneously as if they were members of an orchestra subject to the wand of such an enchanter as Theodore Thomas. What could it be?

For the space ot two or three minutes the silence remained as profound as that of the tomb, and then there came a rush and patter, made by the wolves as they fled pell-mell.

At first sight this seemed a reason for congratulation in getting rid of such unwelcome company; but Fred saw in it more cause for alarm. Very evidently the creatures would not have left the spot in such a hurry unless they were frightened away by some wild animal more to be dreaded than themselves.

"I'm afraid I'll have to use my rifle," he thought, as he moved softly downward until he reached a point from which he could see anything that passed beneath. "It's pretty rough to have to fire a fellow's last shot, when he's likely to starve to death for it; but a beast that can scare away a pack of wolves is likely to be one that will take a well-aimed bullet to stop—"

This train of thought was abruptly checked by a sight which almost paralyzed him. He could dimly discern the ground beneath, and he was watching and listening when a large figure came to view, and halted directly beneath him, where the first wolf had sat upon his haunches and looked so longingly upward.

No noise could be heard and it seemed to move like a phantom; but, even in the gloom, the peculiar swinging motion of the body showed prodigious strength and activity. There could be no doubt, either, that the animal was a climber, and therefore more to be feared than a thousand wolves.

Fred had gained quite a knowledge of the animals of the country on his way across the plains, and in the indistinct view obtained he made up his mind that this was that most dangerous of wild beasts in the Southwest, the American cougar. If such were the case, the lad's only defense lay in the single charge of his rifle. The cougar could leap among the limbs as easily as a cat bounds from the floor into the chair.

Fred had left his rifle beyond his reach, and he was about to climb up to it, when the possibility occurred to him that, perhaps, the cougar was not aware that any one was in the tree, and, if unmolested might pass by. Accordingly, the fugitive remained as motionless as a statue, his eyes fixed upon the dreaded brute, ready to make for his gun the instant the cougar showed any sign of making for him.

The animal, known in some parts of the country as the panther, or "painter," remained equally motionless. It looked precisely as if he suspected that something was in the wind and had slipped up to this point to listen for some evidence of what it was. Fred, who had heard fabulous stories of the "smelling" powers of all wild animals, feared that the cougar would scent him out, but he showed no evidence of his ability to do so.

After remaining stationary a minute or two, he moved forward a couple of steps, and then paused as before. The lad was fearful that this was an indication that he had detected his presence in the tree and was about to make his leap; but, preliminary to doing so, all such animals squat upon their haunches, and pick out a perch at which to aim. This he had not done, and the boy waited for it before changing his own position.

The head of the cougar was close to the trunk of the tree, and he had maintained the attitude hut a few seconds when he started forward again and continued until he vanished from view.

"I hope he is gone," was the wish that came to Fred, as he peered through the leaves, in his effort to catch a glimpse of him.

But the intervening leaves prevented, and he saw him no more.

He remained where he was for some time, on the look-out for the beast, but finally climbed back to his former place, where his gun was within reach, and where he disposed of himself as comfortably as possible.

In less than ten minutes thereafter, the whole pack of wolves were back again. The cougar had departed, and they returned to claim their breakfast. They were somewhat less demonstrative in their manner, as though they did not wish to bring the panther back again.

They were scarcely upon the ground, however, when Fred noticed that it was growing light in the east. The long, terrible night, the most dreadful of his life, was about over, and he welcomed the coming day as the shipwrecked mariner does the approach of the friendly sail.

The light rapidly increased, and in a short time the sun itself appeared, driving the darkness from the mountain and bathing all in its rosy hues.

The wolves seemed to dread its coming somewhat as they did that of the cougar. By the time the morning was fairly upon them, one of them slunk away. Another speedily followed, and it soon became a stampede.

Fred waited awhile, and then peered out. Not a wolf was to be seen, and he concluded it was safe to descend.

He made several careful surveys of his surroundings before trusting his feet on solid ground again. When he found himself there he grasped his rifle firmly, half expecting the formidable cougar to pounce upon him from some hiding-place; but everything remained quiet, and he finally ventured to move off toward the eastward, feeling quite nervous until he had gone a couple of hundred yards, and was given some assurance that no wild beasts held him in sight.

Now that the lad had some opportunity to gather his wits, he paused to consider what was best to do, for with the coming of daylight came the necessity for serious work. His disposition was to return to the ravine, which he had left for the purpose of seeking a sleeping-place, and to press homeward as rapidly as possible. There was no time to be lost, for many a long and wearisome mile lay between him and New Boston.

As was natural, Fred was hungry again, but he resolved to make no attempt to secure food until night-fall, and to spend the intervening time in traveling. Of course, if a camp-fire should come in his way, where he was likely to find any remnants of food, he did not intend to pass it by; but his wish was to improve the day while it lasted. By taking to the ravine again, he entered upon the Apache highway, where he was likely, at any moment, and especially at the sharp turns, to come in collision with the red men, but the advantage was too great to overlook, and he hoped by the exercise of unusual care to keep out of all such peril.

He was on the margin of the plateau, and before returning to the gorge he thought it best to venture upon a little exploration of his own. Possibly he might stumble upon some narrower pass, one unfit for horses, which would afford him a chance of getting out of the mountains without the great risk of meeting his old enemies.

For a short distance, the way was so broken that his progress was slow. He found himself clambering up a ledge of rocks, then he was forced to make his way around some massive boulders, and in picking his way along a steep place, the gravelly earth gave way beneath his weight, and he slid fully a hundred feet before he could check himself. His descent was so gradual that he was not bruised in the slightest, but he was nearly buried beneath the gravel and dirt that came rattling down after him.

"I wish I could travel all the way home that way," he laughed, as he picked himself up. "I would soon get there, and wouldn't have to work very hard, either."

But this was not very profitable work, and when he had quaffed his fill from a small rivulet of icy-cold water, he was conscious of the importance of going forward without any further delay.

"I guess the best thing I can do is to get back in that ravine or pass without any more foolery. It looks as though the way was open ahead yonder."

It was useless to attempt to retrace his steps, for it was impossible to climb up that incline, which came so near burying him out of sight, so he moved forward, with rocks all around him—right, left, in the rear, and in the front. There was considerable stunted vegetation, also, and, as the day was quite warm, and no wind could reach him, he found the labor of traveling with a heavy rifle anything but fun. Still, he had no thought of giving up, or even halting to rest, so long as his strength held out, and he kept it up until he concluded that it was about time that he reached the ravine for which he aimed from the first.

"It must be right ahead, yonder," he said, after pausing to survey his surroundings. "I've kept going toward it ever since I picked myself up, and I know I wasn't very far away."

He had been steadily ascending for a half hour, and he believed that he had nearly reached the level upon which he had spent the night. His view was so shut in by the character of his surroundings, that he could recognize nothing, and he was compelled, therefore, to depend upon his own sagacity.

Fred had enough wit to take every precaution against going astray, for he had learned long since how liable any one in his circumstances was to make such a blunder. He fixed the position of the sun with regard to the ravine, and as the orb was only a short distance above the horizon, he was confident of keeping his "reckoning."

"That's mighty strange!" he exclaimed, when, having climbed up the place he had fixed in his mind, he looked over and found nothing but a broken country beyond. "There isn't anything there that looks like the pass I'm looking for."

He took note of the position of the sun, and then carefully recalled the direction of the ravine with regard to that, and he could discover no error in the course which he had followed. According to the reasoning of common sense, he ought to strike it at right angles. But just then he recalled that the gorge did not follow a straight line. Had it done so, he would have succeeded in what he had undertaken, but it was otherwise, and so he failed.

"I'll try a little more."

With no little labor, he climbed to an eminence a short distance away, where he hoped to gain a glimpse of the promised land; but the most studied scrutiny failed to show anything resembling the pass.

"I'm lost!" he exclaimed, in despair.

CHAPTER XXIII

A PERILOUS PASSAGE

Fred Munson was right. In his efforts to regain the pass by which he had entered the mountains, he had gone astray, and he knew no more in what direction to turn than if he had dropped from the moon. The sun was now well up above the horizon, and he not only had the mortification of feeling that he had lost much precious time, but that he was likely to lose much more.

With the feeling of disappointment came that of hunger, and he questioned himself as to how he was likely to obtain that with which to stave off the pangs of hunger.

"There isn't any use of staying here," he exclaimed, desperately, "unless I want to lie down and die, and I ain't quite ready for that yet. It is pretty sure the ravine ain't straight ahead, so it must be more to one side."

And, acting upon this conclusion, he made quite a change in the direction he was pursuing, moving off to the left, and encouraging himself with the fact that the pass must be somewhere, and he had only to persevere in exploring each point of the compass to reach it at last. His route continued as precipitous and difficult as before, and it was not long before the plague of thirst became greater than that of hunger. But he persevered, hopeful that his wearisome wandering would soon end.

"Halloa! Here I am again."

This exclamation was caused by the sudden arrival upon the edge of a ravine, which, on first thought, he supposed to be the very one for which he was making. But a second glance convinced him of his error, for it was nothing more than a yawn, or chasm, that had probably been opened in the mountains by some great convulsion of nature.

Making his way carefully to the edge, Fred saw that it had a varying depth of fifty to two hundred feet, and a width from a dozen yards to three times as much, its length seemingly too great to be "gone round" by an ordinary traveler. And yet, finding himself confronted by such a chasm, it was perhaps natural that the lad should become more fully pursuaded than ever of the absolute necessity of placing himself upon the opposite side. The more he thought upon it the more convinced did he become, until his disire of passing over became a wild sort of eagerness that would not let him rest.

"I don't believe the pass is more than a hundred yards from the other side, and the two must run nearly parallel, so I am bound to get over in some way."

In the hope that some narrow portion might be found, he made his way with great care along the margin, until fully an hour had been spent in this manner, with a result that could not be called very satisfactory.

"If I could jump about three times as far as I can, I could go across right yonder—helloa! why didn't I notice that before?"

And the words were yet in his mouth, when he started on a run along the margin of the ravine, at the imminent risk of falling in and breaking his neck. He had espied not only a narrower portion of the ravine, but what seemed to be a fallen tree extending from one side to the other.

If such were really the case, what more could he need? He had thought over this matter of the pass being upon the other side, until no doubt at all remained in his mind, and now the discovery that the chasm was bridged caused the strongest rebound from discouragement to hope.

Upon reaching the bridge, he found that it answered his purpose admirably. The width was less than ten yards, although the depth was enough to make him shudder, when he peered down into it.

He flung a stone, and, as it went spinning downward, it seemed to him that many seconds elapsed before it struck the bottom with a dull thud.

But the tree seemed strong enough to answer every purpose, and capable of bearing a weight much greater than his.

The trunk at the largest part was fully a foot in diameter, and the top extended far enough over the opposite edge to prevent any weakness from the thinning out of the branches.

But what astonished Fred more than anything else, was the discovery that the tree had been felled not, by nature, but by man. The trunk had been cut through, clearly and evenly, by some sharp instrument, and beyond question had been used as a bridge before.

"Somebody has been here ahead of me," reflected the lad, as he examined this interesting evidence, "and I don't believe it was an Indian, either. I don't know what could bring a party into this part of the world, but they have been here surely, and if the bridge was good enough for them, it will do for me."

He was quite certain that he could walk over, after the fashion of Blondin, but it would have been foolhardy in the highest degree, and he adopted the wiser course of putting himself astride of the trunk, and hitching along a few inches at a time. His rifle interfered somewhat, but he kept up his progress, pausing a few seconds at the centre of the chasm to look down at the bottom far below him.

"Suppose the tree should break," he exclaimed, in a frightened whisper, "it would be the last of a fellow! No one could drop down there, and save his neck without a parachute. I guess the best thing I can do is to get over as soon as I know how—"

At this juncture, as he was on the point of resuming his onward progress, he noticed a peculiar jar of the log, accompanied by a scratching. Mis first impression was that it came from behind, but, upon turning his head, could see nothing. When, however, he looked forward, the terrible explanation at once appeared.

The head or top of the tree was unusually bushy and luxuriant, and, although a considerable time had elapsed since it had been felled, yet there were a great many leaves clinging to the branches—not enough to afford concealment to any animal fleeing from a hunter. Then Fred first looked in that direction, he failed to see that one of the most dangerous animals of the Southwest was crouching there.

As he looked inquiringly ahead now, he observed a huge American cougar, larger than that of the night before, issuing from among the branches. With his phosphorescent eyes fixed upon the terrified lad, he was stealing slowly along the log, giving utterance to a deep guttural growl, separating his lips as he did so, so as to show his long, white, needle-like teeth, intended for the rending of flesh.

For a moment Fred was transfixed at the sight.

The cougar clearly meant fight, and assumed the offensive without a second's hesitancy. He seemed to have been crouching in the bushes, and calmly awaited the time when the boy should advance too far to retreat.

"I guess I'd better go back!" exclaimed the latter, recovering himself, and beginning his retrograde movement; but a few hitches showed that he could not escape the cougar in this fashion, if he really meant business, and it looked very much as if he did.

The beast had already left the other side, and, like his intended victim, was supported over the chasm by the tree. He had advanced beyond the fork made by the junction of the lowermost branches with the main stem, and was stealing along with an appearance of excessive caution, but really with the certainty of a brute who feels that there is no escape for his prey. He moved slowly, burying his long, sharp claws so deeply in the bark at each step, that his feet seemed to stick as he lifted them again. All the time his large, round eyes, which had a greenish glare like those of a cat, were never removed from the face of the lad, and the guttural growl that came from the lowermost depths of his chest was like the muttering of distant thunder.

It was not until about a dozen feet separated the two that Fred recalled that his case was not so desperate as he had imagined. He held a loaded rifle at his command, and the distance was too short for any mistake to be made in the aim.

"I guess I'll stop *your* fun!" was the exultant exclamation of the lad, as he brought his rifle to his shoulder. "I don't like to throw away a shot on you, but I don't see how it can be helped."

He sighted directly between the eyes. His hand shook a little, and the weapon was heavy, but it was impossible that he should miss.

The cougar continued his slow, cautious advance, apparently unaware or uncaring for the deadly weapon aimed at him.

The distance was very slight between the two when the trigger was pulled, and the heavy bullet, tearing its way through bone and muscle, buried itself in the brain, extinguishing life with the suddenness almost of the lightning stroke. The guttural growl wound up with something like a hoarse yelp, and the cougar made what might be termed his death-leap.

The bound was a tremendous one, carrying him clear up over the head of the lad, who crouched down in affright, expecting him to drop upon his shoulders; but he passed far beyond, dropping upon the trunk of the tree, which he clutched and clawed in his blind, frantic way, without saving himself in the least, and down he went.

Fred was held with a sort of fascination, and had turned his head sufficiently to watch every movement of his victim. Then he started downward, his whitish belly was turned upward, while he continued to beat and claw the air in his death struggles.

As is the tendency of falling bodies, the carcass of the cougar showed an inclination to revolve. It began slowly turning over as it descended, and it must have completed several revolutions when it struck the rocky ground below like a limp bundle of rags, and lay motionless.

The boy, from his lofty perch, watched the form below him for several minutes, but could detect no sign of life, and rightly concluded there was none.

"I wonder whether there are any more there," he exclaimed, hesitating to go backward, while he scrutinized the branches with the keenest kind of anxiety. "I don't see any chance where one could hide, and yet I didn't see that other fellow."

It was hardly possible that he should find a companion to the one he had just slain, and he resumed his hitching forward, making it as deliberate and careful as he could. Clutching the branches, he hurried forward and was soon upon the other side of the chasm which had come so nigh witnessing his death. Without pausing longer he hastened on and was not long in placing himself upon the top of the elevation from which he was so confident of gaining his view of the promised land, as the pass had become to him, now that it seemed so difficult to find, and was so necessary to anything like progress.

But another disappointment awaited him. The most careful scrutiny failed to reveal anything like the ravine, and poor Fred was forced to the conclusion that he was hopelessly lost, and nothing but Providence could bring him through the labyrinth of peril in which he was entangled.

Lieutenant R. H. Jayne

CHAPTER XXIV

A TERRIBLE BED

It was nearly noon, and, having failed so completely in his efforts to regain the pass, Fred determined to devote a little time to procuring food. He was certain that he would soon require it and might postpone his hunt too long. Although now and then he suffered somewhat from want of water, yet it was not for any length of time. There was an abundance of streams and rivulets, and he frequently stumbled upon them, when he had no expectation of doing so. Quaffing his fill from one of these, he rested a few minutes, for he had been laboring unceasingly for hours.

"What a pity a fellow, when he got caught in such a fix as this, wasn't like a camel, so that he might store away enough water to last him a week, and then if he could do the same with what he ate, he needn't feel scared when he got lost like me."

His gun, of course, was as useless to him as a stick, and although in his long tramping it became onerous and oppressive, he had no thought of abandoning it.

"I don't see as there is any chance of killing any animals to eat, and, if I did, I haven't got any matches to start a fire to cook them, so I must get what I want some other way."

He had noticed in his wanderings here and there a species of scarlet berry, about the size of the common cherry, but he refrained from eating any, fearing that they were poisonous. He now ventured to taste two or three, and found them by no means unpleasant to the palate; but, fearful of the consequence, he swallowed but a little, waiting to see the result before going into the eating line any more extensively.

A half hour having passed without any internal disturbance, he fell to and ate fully a pint. There was not much nourishment in them, but they seemed to serve his purpose very well, and when he resumed his wandering, he felt somewhat like a giant refreshed with new wine.

As it seemed useless to lay out any definite line to follow, Fred made no attempt to do so, believing he was as likely to reach the ravine by aimless traveling as by acting upon any theory of his own as to the location of the place he desired to reach. This he continued to do until the afternoon was about half spent. He was still plodding along, with some hope of success, when he became aware of a sickness stealing over him. The thought of the berries, and the fear that he had been poisoned, gave him such a shock that the slight nausea was greatly intensified, and he reclined upon the ground in the hope that it would soon pass over.

Instead of doing so, he grew worse, and he stretched out upon the ground, firmly persuaded that his last hour had came. He was deathly pale, and had he espied a cougar peering over the corner of the rock, he wouldn't have paid him the least attention—no, not if there had been a dozen of them!

What alarmed Fred as much as anything was some of the

accompaniments of his trouble. As he laid his head upon the ground, it seemed to him that he could catch the faint sound of falling water, just as if there was a little cascade a mile away, and the gentle wind brought him the soft, musical cadence. Then, too, when he flung himself upon the ground, it gave forth a hollow sound, such as he had never heard before. Several times he banged his heel against the earth, and the same peculiarity was noticed.

All this the poor fellow took as one of the accompaniments of the poisoning, and as additional proof that he was beyond hope. He rolled upon the ground in misery, and wondered whether he would have his mind about him when the last dreadful moment should come; but after a half hour or more had passed, and he was still himself, he began to feel a renewal of hope.

"It may be that I ate too many of them," he reflected, as he found himself able to sit up, "and there's nothing poisonous about them, after all. If that's so, I've got a good meal, anyway, and know where to get another."

It was nearly dark, and, as he was still weak, he concluded to spend the night where he was.

A rod or so away was a dense clump of bushes, which seemed to offer an inviting shelter, and he gained his feet with the intention of walking to them. He had taken no more than a couple of steps, however, when such a dizziness overcame him that he sank at once to the ground, and stretched out for relief. It was a case of poisoning beyond question, but not of a dangerous nature; and Fred had about time to lie flat when he experienced a grateful relief.

"I guess I'll stay here a while," he muttered, recalling his experience. "I can crawl in among the bushes in the night, if

I find it getting cold, or any rain falls."

Darkness had scarcely descended, when the lad sank into a quiet, dreamless slumber. His rest of the night previous had not been of a refreshing character, and his traveling during the day had been very exhaustive, so that his wearied system was greatly in need of rest.

Fred was really in the most delightful climate in the world. New Mexico is so far south that the heat in many portions, at certain seasons of the year, assumes a tropical fervor. On some of the arid plains the sun's rays have an intensity like that of the Sahara; but numerous ranges of mountains traverse the territory north and south, with spurs in all directions, and the elevation of many of these give a temperature as cool and pleasant as can be desired.

As the lad stretched out upon the ground, he was without a blanket, or any covering except his ordinary clothes; and he needed nothing more. The surrounding rocks shut out all wind, and the air was not warm enough to cause perspiration. The fact was, he had struck that golden mean which leaves nothing to be desired as regards the atmosphere.

The sky remained clear, and, as the moon climbed higher and higher in the sky, it was only at intervals that a fleecy cloud floated before it, causing fantastic shadows to glide over the ground, and making strange phantom-like formations among the mountain peaks and along the chasms, gorges, ravines, and precipices. Had the sleeping lad awoke and risen to his feet, he would have seen nothing of wolf, catamount, or Indian, nor would the straining vision have caught the glimmer of any solitary camp-fire. He was alone in the great solitude, with no eye but the all-seeing One to watch over him.

It was a curious fact connected with the boy's wanderings that more than once he was within a stone's throw of the pass for which he was so anxiously searching; and yet he never suspected it, owing to his unfamiliarity with the territory. As is nearly always the case with an inexperienced hunter, he showed a continual tendency to travel in a circle, the nature of the ground only preventing him from doing so.

Fred slept, without disturbance, until after midnight. An hour or so previous to his waking, when the moon was in the best position to lighten up the earth below, the figure of a man appeared upon an eminence, a hundred yards or more away, and stood motionless for several minutes, as though he were engaged in reverie.

Could one have looked more closely, he would have seen that the stranger's action and manner showed that he was hunting for something. He turned slowly around several times, scanning the ravines, gorges, peaks, and declivities as best he could; but he did not expect to gain much, without the daylight to assist him, and the result of the attempt was anything but satisfactory.

Muttering some impatient exclamation, he turned about and walked slowly away, taking a direction almost the opposite of that which led toward the sleeping boy. He moved with caution, like one accustomed to the wilderness, and was soon lost to view in the gloom.

Then Fred Munson awoke, it was with the impression upon him that he was near some waterfall. He raised his head, but could detect nothing; but when he placed his ear to the ground, he caught it once again.

"I have it!" he said to himself; "there is a waterfall somewhere about here under the ground. That's what makes it sound so hollow when I stamp on it."

He was greatly relieved to find that no results of his afternoon's nausea remained by him. He had recovered entirely, and when he rather doubtingly assumed the sitting position and felt that his head and stomach remained clear he was considerably elated in spirits.

"That shows that I can get a meal at any time, if I want it bad enough to take a few hours' sickness in pay. Maybe I can find something else to eat which won't be so hard on me. It must be very near morning, for I have slept a great while."

The hour, however, was earlier then he supposed, and he found, after sitting awhile, that his old drowsiness was returning.

Before giving way to it, he recalled the clump of bushes, which was so near that it was easily seen from where he sat.

"I forgot that I meant to make my bed there."

With which he rose and moved toward it, not feeling altogether certain of the wisdom of what he was doing.

"That looks very much like the place where the cougar was waiting for me, but I didn't think there were enough in this country to furnish one for every bush."

He reconnoitered it for several minutes, but finally ventured upon a closer acquaintance. There certainly was no wild animal there, and he stooped down and began crawling toward the centre.

He was near the middle when he was alarmed at finding the ground giving way beneath him. It was sinking rapidly downward, and he clutched desperately at the bushes to save himself, but those that he grasped yielded and went, too.

In his terror and despair he cried out, and fought like a madman to save himself; but there was nothing firm or substantial upon which he could lay hold, and he was helpless to check his descent.

Down, down, down he went in the pulseless darkness, lower and lower, until he found himself going through the dizzying air—to where?

CHAPTER XXV

WITHIN THE EARTH

It was like a terrible dream, and, for an instant or more, during which Fred Munson was descending through the gloom and darkness, he believed it was such indeed; but he was quickly recalled from his error by his arrival at the end of his journey. The truth was that the boy, in crawling beneath the clump of bushes for shelter, would have crawled head first into the mouth of the cave, but for the fact that the ground immediately surrounding the opening gave way beneath his weight before he reached it.

His fall was not very far, and when he struck the ground, it was so soft and yielding that he was scarcely conscious of a jar; but the nervous shock was so great that, for a few minutes, he believed that he was fatally injured.

When he was able to recall his scattered senses, he looked around him in the hope of gaining some idea of where he was; but he quickly saw that he was in a place where his eyes were of no service. The darkness was as impenetrable as that which plagued Pharoah and his Egyptians. Only when he looked upward was the blackness of darkness relieved. Enough straggling rays worked their way through the bushes to give the opening a dim, misty appearance, such as is sometimes observed when that orb is rising in a cloud of fog and vapor; but in every other direction he might as well have been blind, for all the good his eyes did him.

One of the first things that struck the lad was the sound of the waterfall which he had heard so distinctly when stretched upon the earth. It was somewhere near him—so close, even, that he fancied he could feel the dampness from it, but the soft, rippling character showed that it did not amount to much. It was a mere cascade, the water of which entered and passed out the cavern by some means which the boy could only surmise.

How extensive was this cave?

Had it any outlet other than that by which Fred had entered? Was the flow even or irregular? Were there pitfalls and abysses about him, making it too perilous to attempt to grope about in the gloom?

Having entered, how was he to make his way out again?

Such questions as these presented themselves to the boy, as he stood alone in a world of night, and endeavored to consider the situation calmly. Stooping down, he felt of the soil. It was of a cold, sandy nature, and so yielding that, when he struck it, he went below his ankles.

He stood for some time, debating whether he should remain where he was until the coming of day, in the hope of gaining additional light, or whether he should venture upon a little cautious exploration. He finally decided upon the latter.

"When the elephant goes on a bridge, he feels of it with his trunk to see whether it is strong enough to bear him, and I'll use my gun to do the same thing."

This was no more than a simple precaution, and doubtless saved his life. Grasping the stock firmly, he reached the muzzle forward, and "punched" the ground pretty thoroughly before venturing upon it, making sure that it was capable of bearing him safely forward into the darkness beyond.

Generally speaking, the ground of the cavern was tolerably even. There were little irregularities here and there, but none of them were of a nature to interfere with walking, provided one could have enough light to see where he was going.

"If I only had a lantern, I could get round this neighborhood a good deal faster than this," he said. "It wouldn't be anything more than fun to explore this cave, which may be as big as the mammoth one of Kentucky."

Up to this time Fred had been moving almost directly away from the cascade which he had noticed. The misty light over his head served somewhat as a guide, and he determined not to wander away from that, which would prevent his getting lost in the bowels of the earth. The boy was quite confident that there was some easy way of getting out of the cave; for if there was none, except by the opening above, then he was in a Bastile, most surely.

It was undoubtedly the cascade which added to this conviction, for it seemed to him more than likely that if the water entered and left the cave, the volume which did so must be of a varying quantity, so that at certain seasons it was capable of carrying a boy with it. This, of course, was extremely problematical, but it was hopeful enough to prevent anything like despair taking possession of the lad as he felt his way around the cavern.

"Every stream finds its way to the daylight after a time, and so must this, and why can't it take a fellow along with it?

That's what I should like to know—"

He paused, with a gasp of amazement, for at that moment the gun went out of his hand as suddenly as if some one in waiting had grasped the muzzle and jerked it away.

But there was no human agency in the matter. While punching the surface, he had approached a vast abyss, and the thrust over the edge was so unexpected that the impulse carried it out of his hand.

As the boy stood amazed and frightened, he heard the weapon going downward, Heaven could only tell where. First it struck one side, and then another, the sound growing fainter and fainter, until at last the strained and listening ear failed to hear it at all. The depth of the opening was therefore enormous, and Fred shuddered to think how nearly he had approached, and by what a hair's breadth he had escaped a terrible death.

At this juncture, the boy suddenly recalled that he had some friction matches in his possession. He was not in the habit of carrying them, but several days before he had carefully wrapped up a half-dozen, with the intention of kindling a fire in the wood near New Boston. From that time until the present he had failed to remember the circumstance, although he had so frequently felt the need of a light.

He found a half-dozen securely wrapped about with a piece of newspaper, and he carefully struck one.

The moment the point flickered into a flame he held it forward and looked downward.

There was the chasm, which came so nigh swallowing him, in the shape of a seam or rent some three or four feet in width. It had the appearance of having been caused by some convulsion of nature, and it extended at right angles to the course he was pursuing, beyond the limit of his vision. If necessary, it could be leaped over, but the explorer deemed it unwise to do so just then.

Now that he had the means at command, Fred decided to look after the cascade, the sound of which was a guide. His gun was irrevocably gone, and his progress, therefore, became the more tedious. Disliking to creep, he adopted the plan of advancing one step, and then groping around awhile with the other foot, before trusting his weight upon it. This consumed considerable time, but it was the only safe course, after what had taken place, and he kept it up until the musical murmur of the waterfall showed that he had approached about as close as possible.

He then struck another match and held it over his head. It told the whole story.

A stream, not more than three or four feet in width, issued from the darkness, and, flowing some distance, went over a ledge of rock. After falling three or four yards, upon some black and jagged rocks, it gathered itself together and resumed its journey into and through the gloom. The tiny flame was unequal to the task of showing where the water entered and left the cave, and, as the boy was straining his eyesight in the hope of discovering something more, the blaze scorched his fingers, he snapped it out.

"That leaves only four," he mused, as he felt of the lucifers, "and I haven't got enough to spare. I can't gain much by using them that way, and so I guess I'll hold on to these, and see whether the daylight is going to help me."

He picked his way carefully along until he was nearly

beneath the opening which had admitted him, where he sat down upon the dry, sandy ground to await the light of the sun.

"I don't suppose it will help much, for the bushes up there will keep out pretty much of the sunlight that might have come through; but I guess I'll have plenty time to wait, and that's what I'll do."

He fell into a sort of doze, lulled by the music of the cascade, which lasted until the night was over. As soon as he awoke, he looked upward to see how matters stood.

The additional light showed that the day had come, but it produced no perceptible effect upon the interior of the cave. All was as dark—that is, upon the bottom—as ever. It was only in the upper portion that there was a faint lighting-up.

Fred could see the jagged edges of the opening, with some of the bushes bent over, and seemingly ready to drop down, with the dirt and gravel clinging to their roots. The opening was irregular, and some four or five feet in extent, and, as near as he could estimate, was some thirty feet above his head.

"If I happened to come down on a rock, I might have got hurt; but things down here were fixed to catch me, and it begins to look as though they were fixed to hold me, too."

His situation was certainly very serious. He had no gun or weapons of any kind other than a common jack-knife, and it looked very much as if there was no way for him to get out the cave again without outside assistance, of which the prospect was exceedingly remote.

He was hungry, and without the means of obtaining food.

The berries, which had acted so queerly with him the day before, were beyond his reach.

Vegetation needs the sunlight, as do all of us, and it is useless to expect anything edible below.

"Unless it's fish," thought Fred, aloud. "I've heard that they find them in the Mammoth Cave without eyes, and there may be some of the same kind here; but then I'm just the same as a boy without eyes, and how am I going to find them?"

The more he reflected upon his situation, the more disheartened did he become. He had been given many remarkable deliverances in the past few days, and although his faith was strong that Providence would bring him out of this last predicament, his heart misgave him as he considered it in all its bearings.

"The best thing I can do is to try and gather some wood together, and start a fire. If there is enough fuel, I may kindle a lantern that will show me something in the way of a new door—Halloa! what is the matter?"

His attention was attracted by the rattling of gravel and dirt at his side, and looking up, he saw that something was struggling in the opening above, having been caught apparently in precisely the same manner as he had been.

His first supposition was that it was a wild animal, but the next moment he observed that it was a person, most probably an Apache warrior. And by the time Fred had learned that much, down came his visitor.

Lieutenant R. H. Jayne

CHAPTER XXVI

A WELCOME VISITOR

Lonely as Fred Munson felt in that dismal cavern, he preferred the solitude to the companionship of an Apache Indian, and, fearful of discovery, he crouched down to wait until he should move away. His involuntary visitor dropped within a few feet of where he was hiding, and Fred tried to hold his breath for fear he might be detected; but the fellow quietly rose and gave expression to his sentiments.

"Begorrah, if I haven't fell through into the cellar, as me grandmither did when she danced down the whole party, and landed on the bottom, and kept up the jig without a break, keep ing time with the one-eyed fiddler above."

Fred could scarcely believe the evidence of his own senses. That was the voice of his old friend, Mickey O'Rooney, or else he was more mistaken than he had ever been in his life. But whatever doubts might have lingered with him were removed by the words that immediately followed.

"It beats the blazes where that young spalpeen can be kaping himself. Me and Misther Simpson have been on the hunt for two days and more, and now when I got on his trail, and found where he'd crawled into the bushes, and I tried to do the same, I crawled into the biggest cellar in the whole world, and I can't find the stairs to walk out again—"

"Helloa, Mickey! Is that you, my old friend?" called out the overjoyed lad, springing forward, throwing his arms about him, and breaking in most effectually upon his meditations.

The Irishman was mystified for a moment, but he recognized the voice, reached down, and placed his arms in turn about the lad.

"Begorrah, if this ain't the greatest surprise of me life, as Mr. O'Spangarkoghomagh remarked when I called and paid him a little balance that I owed him. I've had a hard hunt for you, and had about guv you up when I came down on you in this shtyle. Freddy, me boy, I crave the privilege of axing ye a question."

"Ask me a thousand, if you want," replied the boy, dancing about with delight.

"Are ye sure that it's yoursilf and nobody else? I don't want to make a mistake that'll cause me mortification, and ye must answer carefully."

"I'm sure it is I, Fred Munson."

"Whoop! hurrah!" shouted Mickey, leaping several feet in the air, and, as he came down, striking at once into the Tipperary jig.

The overjoyed fellow kept it up for several minutes, making the cold, moist sand fly in every direction. He terminated the performance by a higher leap than ever, and a regular Comanche war-whoop. Having vented his overflowing spirits in this fashion, the Irishman was ready to come down

Lieutenant R. H. Jayne

to something like more sober common sense. Reaching out, he took the hand of Fred, saying as he did so:

"Let me kaap hold of your flipper, so that I can prevint your drifting away. Now tell me, my laddy, how did you get here?"

"I come down the same way that you did."

"Through the skylight up there? It's a handy way of going down-stairs, the only trouble being that it's sometimes inconvanient to stop so suddint like. Didn't you obsarve the opening till you stepped into it?"

"I didn't see it then. I was near it, asleep, and when I woke up in the night I crawled in under the bushes to shelter myself, when I went through into the cave. How was it you followed?"

"I was sarching for ye, as I've been doing for the last two days and more. I obsarved the hole, for I had the daylight to help me, and I crawled up to take a paap down to see who lived there, when I must have gone too fur, as me uncle obsarved after he had been hung in a joke, and the ground crumbled beneath me, and I slid in. But let me ax you again, are ye much acquainted in these parts? You know I'm a stranger."

"I never was here before. I've looked around all I can, but haven't been able to find how big the cave is. There's a small waterfall, and the stream comes in and goes out somewhere, and there is *one* rent, at least, so deep that I don't believe it has any bottom. I've learned that much, and that's all."

"That's considerable for a laddy like you. Are you hungry?"

"You'd better believe I am."

"Why had I better belave it?" asked Mickey, with an assumption of gravity that it was impossible for him to feel. "If ye give me your word of honor, I'll belave you, because I've been hungry myself, and know how it goes. I have some lunch wid me, and if ye don't faal above ating with common folks, we'll sup together."

"I am so glad," responded Fred, who was indeed in need of something substantial. "I feel weak and hollow."

"Ye shall have your fill; take the word of an Irishman for that. Would you like to smoke?"

"You know I never smoke, Mickey."

"I didn't ax ye that question, but if ye doesn't feel inclined to do the same, I'll indulge myself a little."

The speaker had been preparing his pipe and tobacco while they were talking, and, as he uttered the last words, he twitched the match against the bowl, and immediately began drawing at it.

As the volumes of smoke issuing from his mouth showed that the flame had done its duty, he held the match aloft, and looked down in the smiling, upturned face of the lad, scrutinizing the handsome countenance, as long as the tiny bit of pine held out.

"Yes, it's your own lovely self, as Barney McDougan's wife obsarved, when he came home drunk, with one eye punched out and his head cracked. Do ye know that while I was surveying your swate face I saw something behind ye?"

"No. What was it?" demanded Fred, with a start and shudder, looking back in the darkness.

"Oh! it was nothing that will harm ye: I think there be some bits of wood there that kin be availed of in the way of kindling a fire, and that's what I misses more than anything else, as me mither used to say when she couldn't find the whisky-bottle. Bestir yourself, me laddy, and assist me in getting together some scraps."

The Irishman was not mistaken in his supposition. Groping around, they found quite a quantity of sticks and bits of wood. All of these were dry, and the best kind of kindling stuff that could be obtained. Mickey was never without his knife, and he whittled several of these until sure they would take the flame from a match when he made the essay.

The fire caught readily, and, carefully nursed, it spread until it roared and crackled like an old-fashioned camp-fire. As it rose higher and higher, and the heavy gloom was penetrated and lit up by the vivifying rays, Mickey and Fred used their eyes to the best of their ability.

The cave seemed to stretch away into fathomless darkness in every direction, excepting one, which was toward the waterfall or cascade. This appeared to be at one side, instead of running through the centre. The dark walls could be seen on the other side of the stream, and the gleam and glitter of the water, for some distance both above and below the plunge.

"Do you obsarve anything new?" asked Mickey.

"Nothing more than what I told you," replied Fred, supposing he referred to the extent of the cavern.

"I have larned something," said the man, significantly.

"What's that?"

"Somebody's been here ahead of us."

"How do you know that?"

"I've got the proof. Will you note that, right there before your eyes?"

As he spoke, he pointed to the kindling-wood, or fuel, of which they had collected considerable, while there was plenty more visible around them. Fred was not sure that he understood him, so he still looked questioningly toward him.

"Wood doesn't grow in such places as this, no more than ye can find praties sprouting out of the side of a tea kettle; but then it might have been pitched down the hole above, or got drifted into it without anybody helping, if it wasn't for the fact that there's been a camp-fire here before."

"How do you make that out, Mickey?"

The Irishman stooped down and picked up one of the pieces of wood, which was waiting to be thrown upon the camp fire. Holding it out, he showed that the end was charred.

"That isn't the only stick that's built after the same shtyle, showing that this isn't the first camp-fire that was got up in these parts. There's been gintlemen here before to-day, and they must have had some way of coming and going that we haven't diskivered as yet."

There seemed nothing unlikely in this supposition of Mickey's, who picked up his rifle from where he had left it lying on the ground, and stared inquiringly around in the gloom.

"I wonder whether there be any wild animals prowling around?"

"I don't think that could be; for there couldn't many of them fall through that hole that let us in, and if they did, they would soon die."

"That minds me that you hinted something about feeling the cravings of hunger, and I signified to you that I had something for ye about my clothes; and so I have, if it isn't lost."

As he spoke, he drew from beneath his waistcoat a package, carefully wrapped about with an ordinary newspaper. Gently drawing the covering aside, he displayed a half-dozen pieces of deer-meat, cooked to a turn.

"Will ye take some?" he asked, handing one to Fred, who could scarcely conceal his craving eagerness, as he began masticating it.

"How comes it that you have that by you?"

"I ginerally goes prepared for the most desprit emergencies, as me mither used to remark when she stowed the whisky-bottle away wid the lunch she was takin' with her. It was about the middle of yisterday afternoon that I fetched down a deer that was browsing on the bank of a small stream that I raiched, and, as a matter of coorse, I made my dinner on him. I tried to lay in enough stock to last me for a week—that is, under my waistband—but I hadn't the room; so I sliced up several pieces, rather overcooked 'em, so as to make 'em handy to carry, and then wrapped 'em up in the paper."

"It's a common-sense arrangement," added Mickey. "I had the time and the chance to do it, and it was likely to happen that, when I wanted the next meal, I wouldn't have the same opportunity, remembering which I did as I said, and the result is, I've brought *your* dinner to you."

CHAPTER XXVII

A SUBTERRANEAN CAMP-FIRE

There is no sauce like hunger, and after Fred Munson's experience of partial starvation, and nausea from the wild berries which he had eaten, the venison was as luscious as could be. It seemed to him that he had never tasted of anything he could compare to it.

"Fred, me laddy, tell me all that has happened to you since we met—not that, aither, but since Lone Wolf snapped you up on his mustang, and ran away wid you. I wasn't about the city when the Apaches made their call, being off on a hunt, as you will remember, so I didn't see all the sport, but I heard the same from Misther Simpson."

Thus invited, the boy went over the narration, already known, giving the full particulars of his adventures, from the morning he opened his eyes and found himself in the camp of the Apaches in the mountains; to the hour when he slipped through from the upper earth into the cave below. Mickey listened with great interest, frequently interrupting and expressing his surprise and gratitude at the good fortune which seemed to succeed bad fortune in every case.

"You sometimes read of laddies like you gettin out of the

claws of these spalpeens, but you don't often see it, though you've been lucky enough to get out."

"Now, Mickey, tell me how it was that you came to get on my track."

"Well, you see, I got back to New Bosting shortly after the rumpus. I would have been in time enough to have had a hand in the wind-up, if it hadn't been that I got into a little circus of my own. Me and a couple of Apaches tried the game of cracking each other's heads, that was spun out longer than we meant, and so, as I was obsarving, when I rode into town, the fun was all over. I found Misther Simpson just gettin' ready to take your trail, and he axed me to do the same, and I was mighty glad to do it. I was desirous of bringing along your horse Hurricane, for you to ride when we should get you, but Soot wouldn't hear of it. He said the horse would only be a bother, and if we should lay hands onto you, either of our horses was strong enough to take you, so we left the crature behind."

"Did you have any trouble in following us?"

"Not at first; a hundred red spalpeens riding over the prairie can't any more hide their trail than an Irishman can save himself from cracking a head when he is invited to do so. We galloped along, without ever scarcely looking at the ground. You know I've larned something of the perarie business since we came West, and that was the kind of trail I could have follered wid both eyes shut and me hands handcuffed, and, knowing as we naaded to hurry, we put our mustangs to their best paces."

"How was it that you didn't overtake us?"

"You had too much of a start; but when we struck the camp

in the mountains—that is, where Lone Wolf and his spalpeens took their breakfast—we wasn't a great way behind 'em. We swung along at a good pace, Soot trying to time ourselves so that we'd strike 'em 'bout dark, when he ca'c'lated there'd be a good chance to work in on 'em."

"How was it you failed?"

"We'd worked that thing as nice as anything you ever heard tell on, if Lone Wolf hadn't played a trick on us. We hadn't gone far on the trail among the mountains, when we found that the spalpeens had separated into two parties—three in one, and something like a hundred in the other."

"And you did not know which had charge of me?"

"There couldn't be any sartinty about it, and the best we could do was to make a guess. Soot got off his mustang and crawled round on his hands and knees, running his fingers over the ground, and looking down as careful like as me mither used to do with my head when she obsarved me scratching it more industrious than usual. He didn't say much, and arter a time he came back to where his mustang was waitin', and, leanin' agin the beast, looked up in my face, and axed me which party I thought you was in. I said the thray, of course, and that was the rason why they had gone off by themselves."

"You were right, then, of course."

"Yes, and when I answered, Soot, he just laughed kind o' soft like, and said that that was the very rason why he did not believe you was with the thray. He remarked that Lone Wolf was a mighty sharp old spalpeen. He knowed that Soot would be coming on his trail, and he divided up his party so as to bother him. Anybody would be apt to think just the same as I did—that the boy would be sent to the Injun town in charge of the little party, while the others went on to hatch up some deviltry. Lone Wolf knowed enough to do that, and he had therefore kept the laddy with the big company, maaning that his old friend, the scout, should go on a fool's errand.

"That's the way Soot rasoned, you see, and that's where he missed it altogether. He wasn't ready for both of us to take the one trail, so it was agreed that we should also divide into two parties—he going after the big company and I aiter the small one, he figuring out that, by so doing, he would get all the heavy work to do, and I wouldn't any, and there is where he missed it bad. There wasn't any way that we could fix it so that we could come together again, so the understanding was that each was to go on his own hook, and get back to New Bosting the best way we could, and if there wasn't any New Bosting to go to, why, we was to keep on till we reached Fort Severn, which, you know is about fifty miles beyant.

"You understand, I was just as sartin' that I was on your trail as Soot was that he was gainin' on ye; so we both worked our purtiest. I've been studyin' up this trailin' business ever since we struck this side of the Mississippi, and I'd calculated that I'd larned something 'bout such things. I belave I could hang to the tracks of them three horsemen till I cotched up to 'em, and nothing could throw me off; but it wasn't long before I begun to get things mixed. The trail bothered me, and at last I was stunned altogether. I begun to think that maybe Soot was right, after all, and the best thing I could do was to turn round and cut for home; but I kept the thing up till I struck a trail that led up into the mountains, which I concluded was made by one of the spalpeens in toting you off on his shoulders. That looked, too, as if the Ingin' settlement was somewhere not far off, and I begun to think ag'in that Soot was wrong and I right. I kept the thing up till night, when I hadn't diskivered the first sign, and not only that, but had lost the trail, and gone astray myself."

"Just as I did," Fred observed.

"I pushed my mustang ahead," Mickey continued, "and he seemed to climb like a goat, but there was some places where I had to get off and help him. I struck a spot yesterday where there was the best of water and grass, and the place looked so inviting that I turned him loose, intending to lave him to rist till to-day. While he was there, I thought I might as well be taking observations around there, makin' sartin' to not get out of sight of the hoss, so I shouldn't get lost from him."

"And is he near by?"

"Not more than a mile away. I was pokin' 'round like a thaif in a pratie-patch, when I coom onto a small paice of soft airth, where, as sure as the sun shines, I seed your footprint. I knowed it by its smallness, and by the print of them odd-shaped nails in your heel. Well, you see, that just set me wild. I knowed at once that by some hook or crook you had give the spalpeens the slip, and was wandering round kind of lost like mysilf. So I started on the tracks, and followed them, till it got dark, as best I could, though they sometimes led me over the rocks and hard earth, in such a way that I could only guess at 'em. When night came, I was pretty near this spot, but I was puzzled. I couldn't tell where to look further, and I was afeared of gettin' off altogether. So I contented mesilf wid shtrayin' here and there, and now and then givin' out the signal that you and me used to toot when we was off on hunts together. When this morning arriv', I struck signs agin, and at last found that your track led toward these bushes, and thinks I to myself, thinks I, you'd crawled in there to take a snooze, and I hove ahead to wake you up, but I was too ambitious for me own good, as was the case when I proposed to Bridget O'Flannigan, and found that she had been already married to Tim McGubbins a twelvemonth, and had a pair of twins to boast of. I own it wasn't a dignified and graceful way of coming down-stairs, but I was down before I made up my mind."

"Well, Mickey, we are here, and the great thing now is to get out. Can you tell any way?"

The Irishman took the matter very philosophically. It would seem that any one who had dropped down from the outer world as had he, would feel a trifle nervous; but he acted as if he had kindled his camp-fire on the prairie, with the certainty that no enemy was within a hundred miles.

When he and his young friend had eaten all they needed, there was still a goodly quantity left, which he folded up with as much care in the same piece of paper as though it were a tiara of diamonds.

"We won't throw that away just yet. It's one of them things that may come into use, as me mither used to say when she laid the brickbats within aisy raich, and looked very knowingly at her old man."

After the completion of the meal, man and boy occupied themselves for some time in gathering fuel, for it was their purpose to keep the fire going continually, so long as they remained in the cave—that is, if the thing were possible. There was an immense quantity of wood; it had probably been thrown in from above, as coal is shoveled into the mouth of a furnace, and it must have been intended for the use of parties who had been in the cave before.

When they had gathered sufficiently to last them for a good while, Mickey lit his pipe, and they sat down by the fire to discuss the situation. The temperature was comfortable, there being no need of the flames to lessen the cold; but there was a certain tinge of dampness, natural to such a location, that made the fire grateful, not alone for its cheering, enlivening effect, but for its power in dissipating the slight peculiarity alluded to.

Seated thus the better portion of an hour was occupied by them in talking over the past and interchanging experiences, the substance of which had already been given. They were thus engaged when Mickey, who seemed to discover so much from specimens of the fuel which they had gathered, picked up another stick, which was charred at one end, and carefully scrutinized it, as though it contained an important sermon intended for his benefit.

CHAPTER XXVIII

THE EXPLORING TOUR

After gently tossing the stick in his hand, like one who endeavors to ascertain its weight, Mickey smelled of it, and finally bit his teeth into it, with a very satisfactory result.

"Now, that's what I call lucky, as the old miser observed when he found he was going to save his dinner by dying in the forenoon. Do you mind that shtick—big enough to sarve as a respictable shillalah at Donnybrook Fair? Well, my laddy, that has done duty as a lantern in this very place."

"As a torch, you mean?"

"Precisely; just heft it." As he tossed it into Fred's hand, the latter was astonished to note its weight.

"What's the cause of that?" he inquired.

"It's a piece of pine, and its chuck full of pitch. That's why it's so heavy. It'll burn like the biggest kind of a candle, and me plan, me laddy, is to set that afire, and then start out to larn something about this new house."

Nothing could have suited the boy better. He sprang to his

feet and took the gun from Mickey, so as to leave him free to carry the torch. One end of the latter was thrust into the fire, and it caught as readily as if it were smeared with alcohol. It was a bit of pine, as fat as it could be, and, as a torch, could not have been improved upon.

Then Mickey elevated it above his head, it gave forth a long yellow smoke blaze, which answered admirably the purpose for which it was required.

"I'll take the lead," said he to his young friend, when they were ready to start. "You follow a few yards behind and look as sharp as you can to find out all there is to be found out. You know there is much that depends on this."

There was no possibility of Fred failing to use all his senses to the utmost, and he told his friend to go ahead and do the same.

Mickey first headed toward the cascade, as he had some hope of learning something in that direction. Reaching the base of the falls, they paused a while to contemplate them. There was nothing noteworthy about them, except their location underneath the ground.

The water fell with such a gentle sound that the two were able to converse in ordinary tones when standing directly at the base. Both knelt down and tasted the cool and refreshing element, and then Mickey, torch in hand, led the way up stream again.

Through this world of gloom the two made their way with considerable care. Mickey cherished a lingering suspicion that there might be some one else in the cave besides themselves, in which case he and Fred would offer the best target possible; but he was willing to incur the risk, and, although he moved slowly, it was with a decision to see the thing through, and learn all that was to be learned about the cave. The stream was followed about a hundred yards above the falls, when the explorers reached the point where it entered the cave, and the two made the closest examination possible.

On the way to the point the two had acquired considerable information. The roof of their underground residence had a varying height from the floor of from twenty to fifty feet. The floor itself was regular, but not sufficiently so to prevent their walking over it with comparative ease. The stream was only five or six feet in width and wherever examined was found to be quite shallow. It flowed at a moderate rate, and it entered the cavern from beneath a rock that ascended continuously from the floor to the roof.

"Freddy, my laddy; do you take this torch and walk off aways, so that it will be dark here," said Mickey to his companion.

The latter obeyed, and the man made as critical an examination as he could. His object was to learn whether the water came into the cave from the outer world, or whether its source was beneath the rock. If the former, there was possibly a way out by means of the stream, provided the distance intervening was not too great. Mickey thought that if this distance were passable, there would be some glimmer of light to indicate it. But, when left alone in the darkness, he found that there was not the slightest approach to anything of the kind, and he was compelled to acknowledge that all escape by that direction was utterly out of the question.

Accordingly, he called Fred to him, and they began the descent of the stream. When they reached the falls, they paused below them, and Micky held the torch close to the water, where it was quiet enough for them to observe the bottom.

"Tell me whether ye can see anything resimbling fishes?"

The lad peered into the water a minute, and them caught a flash of silver several times.

"Yes, there's plenty of them!" he exclaimed, as the number increased, and they shot forward from every direction, drawn to the one point by the glare of the torch. "There's enough fish for us, if we can only find some way to get them out."

"That's the rub," said Mickey, scratching his head in perplexity. "I don't notice any fishlines and hooks about here. Howsumever, we can wait awhile, being as our venizon isn't all gone, and we'll look down stream, for there's where our main chance must be."

The Irishman, somehow or other, had formed the idea that the outlet of the water would show them a way of getting out of the cavern. Despite his careless and indifferent disposition, he showed considerable anxiety, as he led the way along the bank, holding the smoking torch far above his head, and lighting up the gloom and darkness for a long distance on every hand.

"When your eye rists on anything interesting, call me attention to the same," he cautioned him.

"I'll be sure to do that," replied Fred, who let nothing escape him.

The scenery was gloomy and oppressive, but acquired a certain monotony as they advanced. The dark water, throwing back the light of the torch; the towering, massive rocks overhead and on every hand; the jagged, irregular roof and floor—these were the characteristics of the scene which was continually opening before and closing behind them. In several places the brook spread out into a slowly flowing pond of fifty or a hundred feet in width; but it maintained its progress all the time.

At no point which they examined did the depth of the water appear greater than three feet, while in most places it was less than that. It preserved its crystal-like clearness at all times, and in all respects was a beautiful stream.

When they had advanced a hundred yards or so, the camp-fire which they had left behind them took on a strange and unnatural appearance. It seemed far away and burned with a pale yellow glare that would have seemed supernatural, had it been contemplated by any one of a superstitious turn.

As near as Mickey could estimate, they had gone over a hundred and fifty yards when the point was reached where the stream gathered itself and passed from view. Its width was no greater than four feet, while its rapidity was correspondingly increased.

After Mickey had contemplated it awhile by the light of the torch, he handed the latter to Fred, and told him to go off so far that he would be left in total darkness. This being done, the man set to work to study out the problem before him.

His theory was that, if the passage of the stream from the cavern to the outside world were brief, the evidence of it could be seen, perhaps, in the faintest tinge of light in the water, The sun was shining brightly on the outside. and unless the stream flowed quite a distance under ground, a portion of the refracted light would reach his eye.

Mickey peered at the base of the rock for a few minutes, and then exclaimed, with considerable excitement:

"Be the powers! but it's there!"

It was dim and faint, as light is sometimes seen through a translucent substance, but he saw it so plainly that there could be no error. When he looked aloft at the impenetrable gloom, he was sensible of the same dim light upon the water. He tested his accuracy of vision by looking in different directions, but the result was the same every time.

The almost invisible illumination being there, the Irishman wanted no philosopher to tell him that it was the sun striking the water as it reached the outside, and the outer world, which he was so desirous of re-entering, was close at hand.

Mickey was in high glee at the discovery, but when he regained his mental poise, he could not shut his eyes to the fact that if he attempted to reach the outer world by means of the stream, he ran a terrible risk of losing his life. There was no vacancy between the water and the stone which shut down upon it. The outlet was like an open faucet to a full barrel. The escaping fluid filled up all the space at command.

No one can live long without air. A few seconds of suspended respiration is fatal to the strongest swimmer. If the distance traveled by Mickey, when he should attempt to dive or float through to the outer world, should prove a trifle too long, the stream would cast out a dead man instead of a live one.

But he was a person of thorough grit, and before he would consent to see himself and Fred imprisoned in this cavern, he would make the attempt, perilous as it was.

Was there no other way of escape? Was there not some opening which had been used by those who had entered this cave ahead of him? Or was it possible that the imprisoning walls were to thin and shell-like in some places that there was a means of forcing their way out? Or was there no plan of climbing up the side of the prison and reaching an opening in the roof, through which they could clamber to safety?

These and other thoughts were surging through the mind of Mickey O'Rooney, when an exclamation from Fred caused him to turn his head. The boy was running toward him, apparently in great excitement.

"What's the matter, me laddy?" asked Mickey, cocking his rifle, which he had taken from him at the time of handing him the torch. "Oh, Mickey, Mickey! I saw a man just now!"

CHAPTER XXIX

A MYSTERY

O'Rooney stood with rifle grasped, while young Munson ran toward him from the centre of the cave, exclaiming in his excited tones:

"There's another man back yonder! I saw him and spoke to him!"

"Did ye ax him anything, and did he make a sensible reply?" demanded the Irishman, whose concern was by no means equal to that of the lad.

"He made no answer at all, nor did he seem to take any notice of me."

"Maybe it's a ghost walking round the cave, on the same errand as meself. But whist now; where is he, that I may go and ax him the state of his health?"

The lad turned to lead the way, while Mickey followed close at his heels, his gun ready to be used at an instant's warning, while Fred kept glancing over his shoulder, to make sure that his friend was not falling too far in the rear.

It seemed that, while the man was engaged in his exploration, the lad had ventured upon a little prowling expedition of his own. During this he made the startling discovery that some one else was in the cave, and he dashed off at once: to notify his friend and guide.

Fred walked some distance further, still holding the torch above his head and peering into the gloom ahead and on either hand, as though in doubt as to whether he was on the right track or not. All at once he stopped with a start of surprise, and, pointing some distance ahead and upon the ground, said:

"There he is!"

Following the direction indicated, Mickey saw the figure of a man stretched out upon the ground, face downward, as though asleep.

"You ain't afeard of a dead spalpeen?" demanded Mickey, with a laugh. "You might have knowed from his shtyle that he's as dead as poor Thompson was when Lone Wolf made a call on him."

"How do you know he's dead?" asked Fred, whose terror was not lessened by the word of his friend.

"'Cause he couldn't have stretched out that way, and kept it up all the time we've been fooling round here. If ye entertain any doubt, I'll prove it. Let me have your torch."

Taking it from the lad's trembling hand, he walked to the figure, stooped down, and, taking it by the shoulder, turned it over upon its back. The result was rather startling even to such a brave man as Mickey. It was not a dead man which the two looked down upon, but practically a skeleton—the remains of an individual, who, perhaps, had been dead for years. Some strange property of the air had dessicated the flesh, leaving the face bare and staring, while the garments seemed scarcely the worse for their long exposure.

Another noticeable feature was the fact that the clothing of the remains showed that not only was he a white man, but also that he was not a hunter or frontier character, such as were about the only ones found in that section of the country. The coat, vest, and trousers were of fine dark cloth, and the boots were of thin, superior leather. The cap was gone. It was just such a dress as is encountered every day in our public streets.

Mickey O'Rooney contemplated the figure for a time in silence. He was surprised and puzzled. Where could this person have come from? There was nothing about his dress to show that he belonged to the military service, else it might have been supposed that he was some officer who had wandered away from his post, and had been caught in the same fashion as had the man and boy.

"Are there any more around here?" asked Mickey, in a subdued tone, peering off into the gloom.

Fred passed slowly round in a circle, gradually widening out, until he had passed over quite an area, but without discovering anything further.

"There isn't any one else near us. If there is, he is in some other part of the cave."

"How came ye to find this fellow?"

"I was walking along, never thinking of anything of the kind, when I came near stepping upon the body. I was never more scared in my life."

"That's the way wid some of yees—ye're more affrighted at a dead man than a live one. Let's see whether he has left anything that ye can identify him by."

Upon examining further, a silver-mounted revolver was found beneath the body. It was untarnished, and seemingly as good as the day it was completed. When Mickey came to look at it more closely, he found that only one barrel had been discharged, all the others being loaded.

This fact aroused a suspicion, and, looking again at the head, a round hole, such as would have been made only by a bullet, was found in the very centre of the forehead. There could be but little doubt, then, that this man, whoever he was, had wandered about the cavern until famished, and, despairing of any escape, had deliberately sent himself out of the world by means of the weapon at his command. But who was he?

Laying the handsome pistol aside, Mickey continued the search, anxious to find something that would throw light upon the history of the man. It was probable that he had a rifle—but it was not to be found, and, perhaps, had vanished, as had that of Fred Munson. It was more likely that something would be found in his pockets that would throw some light upon the question; and the Irishman, having undertaken the job, went through it to the end.

It was not the pleasantest occupation in the world to ransack the clothing of a skeleton, and he who was doing it could not help reflecting as he did so that it looked very much like a desecration and a robbing of the dead. To his great disappointment, however, he failed to discover anything which would give the slightest clue. It looked as if the man had purposely destroyed all such articles before destroying himself, and, after a thorough search, Mickey was compelled to give up the hunt.

Five chambers of the revolver, as has be said, were still loaded, and, after replacing the caps, the new owner was confident they were good for that number of shots.

"Here," said he, handing the weapon to the boy; "your rifle is gone, and you may as well take charge of this. It may come as handy as a shillelah in a scrimmage, so ye does hold on to the same."

Fred took it rather gingerly, for he did not fancy the idea of going off with property taken from a dead man, but he suffered his friend to pursuade him, and the arrangement was made.

In the belief that there might be others somewhere around, Mickey spent an hour or two longer in an exploration of the cave, with the single purpose of looking for bodies. They approached the ravine in which Fred had dropped his gun. The Irishman leaped across, torch in hand, and prosecuted his search along that side; but they were compelled to give over after a time and conclude that only a single individual had preceded them in the cave.

"Where he came from must iver remain a mystery," said Mickey. "He hasn't been the kind of chaps you find in this part of the world; but whoever he was, it must have been his luck to drop through the skylight, just as we did. He must have found the wood here and kindled a fire. Then he wint tramping round, looking for some place to find his way out, and kept it up till he made up his mind it was no use Then he acted like a gintleman who preferred to be shot to starving, and, finding nobody around to 'tend to the business, done it himself."

"Can't we bury him, Mickey?"

"He's buried already."

The Irishman meant nothing especial in his reply, but there was a deep significance about it which sent a shudder through his hearer from head to foot. Yes, the stranger was buried, and in the same grave with him were Mickey O'Rooney and Fred Munson.

The speaker saw the effect his words produced, and attempted to remove their sting.

"It looks very much to me as if the man hadn't done anything but thramp, thramp, without thrying any way of getting out, and then had keeled over and give up."

"What could he do, Mickey?"

"Couldn't he have jumped into the stream, and made a dive? He stood a chance of coming up outside, and if he hadn't, he would have been as well off as he is now."

"Is that what *you* mean to do?"

"I will, before I'd give up as he did; but it's meself that thinks there's some other way of finding our way. Bring me gun along, and come with me!"

Mickey carried the torch, because he wished to use it himself. He led the way back to where the stream disappeared from view, and there he made another careful examination, his purpose being different from what it had been in the first place. He stooped over and peered at the dark walls, noting the width of the stream and the contour of the bank, as well as the level of the land on the right. Evidently he had some scheme which he was considering.

He said nothing, but spent fully a half hour in his self-imposed task, during which Fred stood in the background, trying to make out what he was driving at. He saw that Mickey was so intently occupied that he was scarcely conscious of the presence of any one else, and he did not attempt to disturb him. Suddenly the Celt roused himself from his abstraction, and, turning to the expectant lad, abruptly asked:

"Do you know, me laddy, that it is dinner-time?"

"I feel as though it was, but we have no means of judging the time, being as neither of us carries a watch."

"Come on," added the Irishman, leading in the direction of the camp-fire. "I'm sorry I didn't bring my watch wid me, but the trouble was, I was afeard that it might tire out my horse, for it was of goodly size. The last time it got out of order, it took a blacksmith in the owld country nearly a week to mend it. It was rather large, but it would have been handy. Whenever we wanted to cook anything, we could have used the case for a stew-pan, or we could have b'iled eggs in the same, and when we started our hotel at New Boston, it would have done for a gong. It was rather tiresome to wind up nights, as the key didn't give you much leverage, and if your hold happened to slip, you was likely to fall down and hurt yersilf. But here we are, as Jimmy O'Donovan said when he j'ined his father and mother in jail."

CHAPTER XXX

DISCUSSIONS AND PLANS

When they reached the camp-fire, it had burned so low that they threw on considerable more wood before sitting down to their lunch. As it flamed up and the cheerful light forced the oppressive gloom back from around them, both felt a corresponding rise in spirits.

"It was lucky that I brought along that maat," remarked Mickey, as he produced the venison, already cooked and prepared for the palate. "It's a custom that Mr. Soot Simpson showed me, and I like it very much. You note that the maat would be a great deal better if we had some salt and pepper, or if we could keep it a few days till it got tender; but, as it is, I think we'll worry it down."

"It seems to me that I never tasted anything better," responded Fred, "but that, I suppose, is because I become so hungry before tasting it."

"Yees are right. If ye want to know how good a cup of water can taste, go two days without drinking; or if ye want to enjoy a good night's rest, sit up for two nights, and so, if ye want to enjoy a nice maal of victuals, ye must fast for a day or two. Now, I don't naad any fasting, for I always enjoyed ating from the first pratie they giv me to suck when I was a few waaks old."

"Well, Mickey, you've been pretty well around the cave, and I want to know what you think of our chance of getting out?"

"The face of the Irishman became serious, and he looked thoughtfully into the fire a moment before answering. Disposed as he was to view everything from the sunshiny side, Mickey was not such a simpleton as to consider their incarceration in the cave a matter that could be passed off with a quirp and jest. He had explored the interior pretty thoroughly, and gained a correct idea of their situation, but as yet he saw no practical way of getting out. The plan of diving down the stream, and trusting to Providence to come up on the outside was to be the last resort.

Mickey did not propose to undertake it until convinced that no other scheme was open to him. In going about the cave, he struck the walls in the hope of finding some weak place, but they all gave forth that dead sound which would have been heard had they been backed up by fifty feet of solid granite. Among the many schemes that he had turned over in his mind, none gave as little promise as this, and he dismissed it as utterly impracticable.

He could conjure no way of reaching that opening above their heads. He could not look up at that irregular, jagged opening without thinking how easy it would be to rescue them, if they could make their presence known to some one outside. There was Sut Simpson, who must have learned that he had gone upon the wrong trail, and who had, therefore, turned back to the assistance of his former comrade.

The latter knew him to be a veteran of the prairie, one who could read signs that to others were like a sealed book, and whose long years of adventure with the tribes of the Southwest had taught him all their tricks; but whether he would be likely to follow the two, and to understand their predicament, was a question which Mickey could not answer with much encouragement to himself. Still there was a possibility of its being done, and now and then the Irishman caught himself looking up at the "skylight," with a longing, half-expectant gaze.

There were several other schemes which he was turning over in his mind, none of which, however, had taken definite shape, and, not wishing to discourage his young friend, he answered his question as best he could.

"Well, my laddy, we're going to have a hard time to get out, but I think we'll do it."

"But can you tell me how?"

Mickey scratched his head in his perplexed way, hardly feeling competent to come down to particulars.

"I can't, exactly; I've a good many plans I'm turning over in my head, and some of them are very fine and grand, and its hard to pick out the right one."

Fred felt that he would like to hear what some of them were, but he did not urge his friend, for he suspected that the fellow was trying to keep their courage up.

They had finished their meal, and were sitting upon the sandy soil, discussing the situation and throwing an occasional longing look at the opening above. They had taken care to avoid getting directly beneath it; for they had no wish to have man or animal tumble down upon their heads. Now and then some of the gravel loosened and rattled down, and the clear light that made its way through the overhanging bushes showed that the sun was still shining, and, no doubt, several hours still remained to them in which to do any work that might present itself. But, unfortunately, nothing remained to do.

Whatever were the different schemes which Mickey was turning over in his mind, none of them was ripe enough to experiment with. As the Irishman thought of this and that, he decided to make no special effort until the morrow. He and Fred could remain where they were without inconvenience for a day or two longer, but it was necessary, too, that they should have their full strength of body and mind when the time should come to work.

"Sometimes when I git into a sore puzzle," said Mickey, "and so many beautiful and irritating plans come up before me that I cannot find it in my heart which way to decide, I goes to slape and drames me way through it, right straight into the right way."

"Did you ever find your path out of trouble?" inquired Fred.

"Very frequently—that is, not to say so frequently—but on one or two important occasions. I mind the time when I was coorting Bridget O'Flaherty and Mollie McFizzle, in the ould counthry. Both of 'em was fine gals, and the trouble was for me to decide which was the best as a helpmate to meself.

"Bridget had red hair and beautiful freckles and a turn-up nose, and she was so fond of going round without shoes that her feet spread out like boards; Molly was just as handsome, but her beauty was of another style. She had very little hair upon her pad, and a little love-pat she had wid an old beau of hers caused a broken nose, which made her countenance quite picturesque. She was also cross-eyed, and when she cocked one eye down at me, while she kept a watch on the door wid the other, there was a loveliness about her which is not often saan in the famale form."

"And you couldn't decide which of these would make you the best wife?"

"Nary a once. The attraction of both was nearly equal."

"But how about their housekeeping? I've often heard father tell what a splendid housekeeper mother was, and how he would rather have his wife a good housekeeper than beautiful."

"But the trouble was, I had both. I've described you the charms and grace of each, and when I add that both were elegant housekeepers, ye'll admit that my dilemma was greater than ever. They both handled the broom to perfection; they could knock a chap clane across the cabin and out of the window before ye could know what was coming. Me mither used to say it was the housekeeping qualities that should decide, and she told me to call upon 'em sometime when they wasn't expecting me, and obsarve the manner in which they handled things. Wal, Bridget was the first one that I sneaked in upon. I heard a thumping noise as I drew near, as though something was tumbling about the floor, and when I peeped through the door, I saw that Bridget and her mother was havig a delightful love-pat. They was banging and whaling each other round the room, and, as the old lady had her muscle well up, it was hard to tell which was coming out ahead. Of course, my sympathies were with the lovely Bridget, and I was desirous that she should win— but I didn't consider it my duty to interfere. I supposed the old lady had been trying to impose too much work on Bridget, and, therefore, she had rebelled, and was lambasting her for the same. My interest in the little affair was so great, that I pushed the door ajar, and stood with me mouth and eyes wide open. It wasn't long before I began to get worried, for, from the way things looked, the owld lady was getting the upper hand. I was thinking I would have to sail in and lend a helping hand, when Bridget fotched the old lady a whack that made her throw up the sponge. Wid that I felt so proud that I sung out a word of encouragement, and rushed forward to embrace my angel, but, before I could do so, she give me a swipe that sent me backward through the door, busting it off, and I was out of the ring.

"The interview was very satisfactory," continued Mickey, "and I wint over to take a sly paap at Molly. As I drawed near the little hut on the edge of the wood, I didn't hear any such noise as I noticed over at Bridget's house. All was as still as it is here this minute. Me first thought was that they all had gone away, but when I got nearer, I noted my mistake. Molly's mother was busy sewing, and sitting near her was her charming daughter Molly, leaning back in her chair, with her head thrown still further back, her mouth wide open, and she a-snoring. I've no doubt that she had become exhausted from overwork, and was taking a little nap. The mother looked up as I stepped softly in, and I axed her, in an undertone, how long her pet child had been asleep. She said between two or three hours, and that she would wake her up, if Molly hadn't told her before closing her eyes that if she dared to disturb her before her nap was finished, she'd break the old lady's head. Knowing the delicate relations that existed betwaan us, she suggested that I should arouse her, she being afraid that she would sleep so long that she would starve to death before she awoke. I wanted to come at the matter gintly, so I took a straw and tickled Molly's nose. She snorted a little, and rubbed it with her fist, but didn't open her eyes. I'd undertook the job, however, and I was bound to do it, or die. So I wiggled at her nostrils, and she made a yell and a jump, and was wide awake. I don't mind me all that took place just then. Things was kind of confused, and, when Molly lit on me, I thought the cabin had tumbled in. My senses came back arter a while, and when I got my head bandaged up, I wint home to dream over it."

"And what was your dream?" asked Fred.

"In my slumbers, I saw both my loves going for each other like a couple of Kilkenny cats, until there was nothing of aither lift. I took that as a sign that naither of 'em was interested for me, and so I give them up, sneaking off and sailing for Ameriky before they learned my intintions."

CHAPTER XXXI

AN EXCHANGE OF SHOTS

Mickey proposed to act upon his own suggestion, which was to go to sleep as soon as the day ended and discuss the many different plans during his slumbers. He had a strong hope that the right one could be hit upon by this method. Somehow or other, his thoughts were fixed upon the stream, where it disappeared under the rocks, and, leaving Fred by the camp-fire, he relit his torch and went off to make another survey.

The lad watched the star-like point of light flickering in the gloom as his friend moved along, holding the torch over his head. It seemed to the watcher that when it paused they were separated by nearly a half mile. The light had an odd way of vanishing and remaining invisible for several minutes that made him think that some accident had befallen the bearer, or that the light had gone out altogether; but after a time it would reappear, dancing about in a way to show that the bearer was not idle in his researches.

Mickey O'Rooney was indeed active. After making his way to the point he was seeking, he shied off to the right, and approached the chasm, down which Fred had lost his rifle. As he stood on the edge of the rent in the fathomless darkness, he loosened a boulder with his foot, and as it toppled over, listened for the result. The way was so narrow that it bounded like a ball from side to side, and the Irishman heard it as it went lower and lower, until at last the strained ear could detect nothing more. There was no sound that came to him to show that it had reached the bottom.

"I s'pose it's going yet," reflected Mickey, after listening several minutes, "and no doubt it will kaap on till it comes out somewhere in Chiny, which I've been told is on t'other side of the world. Now, why couldn't we do the same?" he asked himself, with a sharp turn of the voice. "If that stone is on its way to Chiny, why can't we folly on after it? If we can't reach the crust of the world at this point, what's to hinder our going round by Chiny?—that's what I'd like to know. I wonder how long it would take us? I s'pose we'd get up pretty good steam, and go faster and faster, so that we wouldn't be many days on the road.

"But there's one great objection," he added, scratching his head and knitting his brow with thought. "There's nothing to stop us from bouncing from side to side like that stone. If the way is rough, we'd be pretty sartin to get our breeches pretty well ripped off us, and by the time we raiched Chiny, we wouldn't be in a condition to be presented in coort; and then, too, I haven't enough money about me to pay my way home again."

The visionary scheme was one of those which grew less in favor the more he reflected upon it, and, after turning it over for some minutes longer, he was naturally compelled to abandon the idea.

"I must try the stream agin," he said, as he rose to his feet and groped his way back. "That seems to be the best door, after all, though it ain't the kind I hanker after."

He thrust one end of the torch in the ground some distance away, and walked to the bank close to the great rock beneath which the stream dove and disappeared. Stooping down, he observed the same dull, white appearance that had caught his eye in the first place. Beyond question this was caused by the sunlight striking the water from the outside.

"I could almost swear that a feller wouldn't have to go more than twenty feet before he'd strike daylight," mused Mickey, as he folded his arms and looked thoughtfully at the misty relief of the surrounding darkness; "and it wouldn't take much more to persuade me to make the dive and try it."

As Mickey stood there, contemplating as best he could the darkly flowing stream, and debating the matter with himself, he was on the very eve of making the attempt fully half a dozen times. It seemed to him that he could not fail, and yet there was something in the project which held him back.

The stream at that point flowed quite rapidly, and the strongest swimmer, after venturing a few feet under water, would be utterly unable to return. Once started, there would be no turning back, so he concluded not to make the decisive trial just yet.

"The day is pretty nearly ended, and I will drame over it. I told me laddy that that was my favorite way of getting out of such a scrape, and I'll thry it. If there's no plan that presints itself by to-morrow, then I'll thry it then or the day after."

Going to where his torch was still burning in the sand, he drew it out and moved back toward his old camp-fire.

"Well, me laddy, how have you made out during me absince? Have you—"

He paused and looked about him.

"Begorrah, but no laddy is here. Can it be that he has strayed off, and started to Chiny so as to head me off? I say! Fred, me laddy, have ye—"

"Sh! sh!"

And as the hurried aspirate was uttered, the boy came running silently out of the darkness, with his hand raised in a warning way.

"What is it?" asked Mickey, in amazement; "have ye found another dead man?"

"No; he's a live one!"

"What do yez mane? Explain yerself."

The lad pointed to the opening over their heads, and motioned to his friend not to draw too near the camp-fire. There was danger in doing so.

"There's somebody up there," he added, "and they're looking for us."

"Are ye sure of that?" asked the Irishman, not a little excited at the news. "It may be that Soot Simpson has found us. Begorrah, if there isn't any mistake about it, as me uncle remarked, when he heard that the ship with his wife on was lost at saa, then I'll execute the Donnybrook jig in the highest style of the art. What was it that aroused your suspicion that some jintleman was onmannerly enough to be paaping down on us?"

"I was sitting here watching you, or rather your torch, and all the time the gravel kept rattling down faster and faster, till I knowed there was something more than usual going on up there, and I sneaked away from the fire, where I could get a better look. I went right under the place, and was about to see something worth seeing, when some dirt dropped plump into my eye, and I couldn't see anything for a while. After I had rubbed the grit out I took another look, and I know I saw something moving up there."

"What did it look like?" asked Mickey, who was moving cautiously around, with his gaze fixed upon the same opening.

"I couldn't tell, though I tried hard to get a glimpse. It seemed to me that some one had a stick in his hand, and was beating around the edges of the opening, as though he wanted to knock the loose dirt off. I could see the stick flirted about, and fancied I could see the hand that was holding it, though I couldn't be certain of that."

"No; that's a leetle too much, as me mither obsarved, when me brother Tim said that he and meself had got along a whole half day without fighting, and then she whaled us both for lying. Ye couldn't tell a man's hand at that distance, but I see nothing of him, and I should like ye to tell me where he's gone."

"That is what puzzles me. Maybe he is afraid that we will see him."

Mickey was hardly disposed to accept such an explanation. It seemed to him more likely that it was some wild animal mousing around the orifice, and displacing the dirt with his paws, although he couldn't understand why an animal should be attracted by such a spot.

"It may be one of the spalpeens that got us into all this trouble," he added, still circling slowly about, with his eyes fixed upon the opening. "Those Apaches are sharp-eyed, and perhaps one of their warriors has struck our trail, and tracked us to that spot. If it's the same, then I doesn't see what he is to gain by fooling round up there. If he'd be kind 'nough to let a lasso down that we could climb up by, there'd be some sinse in the same, but—"

To the horror of both, at that instant there was a flash at the opening over their heads, a dull report, and the bullet buried itself in the very centre of the camp-fire.

"Begorrah, but that's what I call cheek, as Ned McGowan used to say when the folks axed him to pay his debts. While we are looking about, and axing ourselves whether there's anybody else at all around us, one of the spalpeens sinds his bullet down here, coming closer to us than is plaisant. Did ye obsarve him?"

"I saw nothing but the flash. Do you think they could see us?"

"Not where we are now. We're too far away from the light. They've seen the fire, and be that token they've concluded that we must be somewhere near it."

"But there was but one shot. Why not more?"

"We'll get the rest of thern arter awhile. That's a sort of faaler, thrown out to see how we take it, as Larry O'Looligan used to say when he knocked a man down. Now, do ye stand aside, and I'll answer 'em."

"You'd better not," protested Fred. "They can tell where we are by the flash of our guns."

"Whisht, now, can't we move? Kape back in the dark like."

The lad moved away several steps, and Mickey, who made sure that his form was not revealed by the light of his own camp-fire, circled around to the other side of the opening, which he was watching with the keenest interest. His purpose was to catch a glimpse of the wretch who had fired the shot. But that seemed about impossible. He could detect something moving now and then, and once or twice there was a twinkle of something red, like the eagle feather in the hair of the warrior, but he could make out nothing definitely.

"He's there; and all I want to do is to be certain of hitting him," he muttered, as he held the cocked rifle to his shoulder. "I'm afeard that if I miss he'll take such good care of himself that I won't get another chance—"

"There, Mickey, there's something," broke in Fred, who was scrutinizing the opening as closely as he could. "Fire, quick! or you won't get the chance!"

The words were scarcely uttered, when the Irishman, who had already taken aim, pulled the trigger, instantly lowering his piece to watch the result.

Both he and Fred fancied they heard an exclamation, but they could not be certain. There was no perceptible commotion about the skylight, but the flickering, erratic movement which had puzzled them ceased on the instant. Whether the shot had accomplished anything or not could only be conjectured, but Mickey was of the opinion that the exchange was equally without result in both cases.

CHAPTER XXXII

FOOTSTEPS IN THE DARKNESS

The direct result of this exchange of shots was to make the two parties more cautious. Mickey and Fred kept further away from the camp-fire, which they suffered to die out gradually. There was really no need fot it, and, since its presence meant danger, it was only prudent to dispense with it altogether.

For fully a half hour not the slightest movement or disturbance at the opening betrayed the presence of any one there, although there could be no doubt that their enemies were within call.

"I can't see what they can gain by loafing around them parts, as the lassies used to obsarve in the ould country when any of the laddies tried to cut me out wid 'em. They needn't watch for us to come out that way, for there ain't much danger of our trying to steal out of that hole—"

"Holloa! Look there!" exclaimed Fred, in considerable excitement; "some of them are coming down to catch us."

Mickey had already noticed that something unusual was up, and, just as the lad spoke, the figure of what seemed to be a

Lieutenant R. H. Jayne

man blocked up the opening, and then began slowly descending, as if supported by a rope, with which his friends were lowering him into the lower room. His form was swathed with a blanket, and there was a certain majesty in the slowly sinking figure, which would have been very impressive but for the fact that it was hardly started when the thin cord by which it was suspended began to twist and untwist, causing the form to revolve forward and backward in a way that was fatal to dignity.

On the impulse of the moment, the Irishman had raised his gun to fire the moment his eyes rested upon the figure. But he restrained himself, not a little puzzled to guess the meaning of such a proceeding. The man, as they believed him to be, was slowly lowered, until something like a dozen feet below the opening, where those who had him in charge seemed to think was the proper place to hold him on exhibition for a time.

"Are you going to shoot?" asked the boy, who did not understand the delay.

"What's the use?" he asked, with an expression of disgust.

"Why, it will stop the man coming down on us."

"Man, do ye say? He ain't any more a man than me gun is."

"What, then, can he be?"

"He's a blanket that they've twisted up so as to look as though it is gathered about the shoulders of an Apache. It's easy to see that there's nothing in it from the way it swings around, as though it was a little toy; and, be the same token, that little cord which holds him aloft is no thicker than a darning-needle. Why they are thrying such a simple thrick is more than I can tell."

"I think I know," said Fred. "They've dropped him down to find out whether we're on the watch or not. If we didn't pay any attention to it, they would think that neither of us was on the look-out, and they would send some others down to scalp us."

"Be the powers, me laddy, I b'lave ye are right!" exclaimed Mickey, admiringly. "That's just the plan of the spalpeens, by which towken, I'll tip him a shot."

With this he raised his rifle, and, sighting rather carelessly, fired. The shot, which was aimed at the roll of blanket, missed it altogether and cut the string which held it suspended in mid-air.

The next moment there was a dull thump upon the sand, and the package lay at the feet of the Irishman, who gave it a kick to make sure of its nature. It rebounded several feet, the resistance to the blow showing that there was nothing more than the simple blanket, and then he stooped over and examined it more closely by the sense of touch.

"'Twas very kind of the spalpeens to furnish us with a blanket that saams as good as this, though the weather ain't so cold that we naad it just now; but sometimes the rain comes and the northers blow, and then a chap is mighty glad to have seech a convanient article about. 'Twas very kind I say."

The result of the little experiment upon the part of the Apaches, it was apparent, was not satisfactory to them. The boy was right in his surmise of its purpose; but it cannot be supposed that they counted upon losing the blanket under any circumstances. It was a costly and beautiful one, such as are made by the Indians of the southwest, and it was new enough to be clean, so that the two fugitives had secured a prize. At all events, the Apaches must have concluded that the people below were keeping watch and ward so well that no one could descend into the cave without danger of being perforated by a rifle ball.

Shortly after this occurrence it began to grow dark above, but the cause was obvious. The day was drawing to a close. Darkness, only less profound than that within the cave below, was enwrapping the surface above.

As soon as the night had fairly descended, Mickey O'Rooney, handling a small torch with great care, made his way once more to the puzzling outlet of the underground stream. The inspection satisfied him of the accuracy of his theory. Not the slightest tinge of light relieved the impenetrable gloom. Mickey considered this strong proof that it was but a short distance to the free air outside, and his courage rose very nearly to the sticking point of making the experiment then and there.

"But we both naad sleep," he mused, as he threw down his torch, and made his way back by the dull glare of the expiring camp-fire. "We both lost considerable last night, and a chap can't kaap reg'lar hours any more than he can when he's coorting three lassies at the same time, and thrying to kaap aich from suspecting it. I faal as though we shall have something lively to do to-morrow, and so we'd better gain all the slumber we kin."

When he reached the camp, he found the lad anxiously awaiting his return. They had signaled to each other several times, but the presence of the danger overhead rendered the boy more uneasy than usual when they were apart.

"Have ye observed nothing?" asked Mickey, in an undertone.

"Nothing at all."

"It's too dark I know, to see, but mebbe yees have heerd something to tell ye that the spalpeens are up there still."

"You may be sure I listened all I know how, but everything has kept as still as the grave. I haven't heard the fall of a pebble even. What do you think the Indians mean to do?"

"Well it's hard to tell. It fooks as though they didn't think we fell in, but had come down on purpose, and had some way of getting out as easy, and they're on the look out for us."

"Maybe, Mickey, there's some other way of coming in, that we haven't been able to find."

"I hoped so a while ago, but I've guv it up. If them spalpeens knowed of any other way, what do they mean by fooling around that place up there, where they're likely to get shot if they show themselves, and they're likely to lose the best blankets they've got?"

Fred did not feel competent to answer this question, and so he was forced to believe that Mickey was right in his conclusion that there was no other way of entering the cave than by the skylight above.

"Which the same thing being the case, I propose that we thry and see how the new blanket answers for a bed. Begorrah! but its fine, as me mither used to say when she run her hands over the head of me dad, and felt the lumps made by the shillelah."

And, having spread the blanket out in the dark-ness, he

rubbed his hands over its velvety surface, admiring its wonderful texture. The texture is such that water can be carried in these Apache blankets with as much certainty as in a metal vessel. But Fred protested against both lying down to sleep at the same time. He thought it likely that the Apaches meant to visit the cave during the night; but his friend laughed his fears to scorn, assuring him that there could be no danger at all. In view of the reception tendered the blanket, the Apaches would take it for granted that the parties beneath were too vigilant to permit anyone to steal a march upon them.

Mickey at once attested his sincerity by stretching out upon the inviting couch, and Fred concluded at last to join him. It was not long before the Irishman was sound asleep, but the lad lay awake a long time, looking reflectively up at the spot where he knew the opening to be,—the opening which had been the means of letting himself and comrade down into that dismal retreat of solitude,—and wondering what their enemies were doing.

"They must know that I am here. Lone Wolf will punish them if they don't keep me, so I am sure they will do all they can to catch me again. I wish I was certain that there was no way of getting in but through that up there, and then I could sleep too, but I feel too scared to do it now."

This anxiety kept him awake a long time after Mickey became unconscious; but, as hour after hour passed and the stillness remained unbroken, his fears were gradually dissipated and a feeling of drowsiness began stealing over him.

Before consciousness entirely departed, he turned upon his side, that being the posture he generally assumed when asleep. As he made the movement and his ear was placed against the blanket, which in its turn rested upon the ground, he heard something which aroused his suspicions instantly and he raised his head. But when he rested on his hands, with his shoulders thrown up, he could hear nothing at all. The earth was a better conductor of sound than the atmosphere, which accounted for what at first seemed curious.

The boy applied his ear as before, and again he heard the noise, faintly, but distinctly; As the eye was of no use, he pressed his head against the blanket and listened. Several minutes were occupied in this manner, and then he said, in an undertone:

"I know what it is!—it is somebody walking as softly as he can. There is another way of getting into this cavern, and those Apaches have found it out. They've got inside and are hunting for us!"

Lieutenant R. H. Jayne

CHAPTER XXXIII

WHAT THE FOOTSTEPS MEANT

Careful listening convinced Fred that there were two red-skins groping around in the darkness. After making himself certain on that point, he reached his hand over, and, grasping the muscular arm of Mickey O'Rooney, shook his companion quite vigorously.

Fred was afraid that, in waking, the Irishman would utter some exclamation, or make such a noise that he would betray their location. When, therefore, several shakings failed to arouse him, the boy easily persuaded himself that it was best to leave him where he was for a time.

"I can tell when they come too close," he reflected, "and then I will stir him up."

A few minutes later he found that he could hear the noise without placing his ear against the blanket; so he lay flat on his face, resting the upper part of his body upon his elbows, with his head thrown up. He peered off in the gloom, in the direction whence the footsteps seemed to come, looking with that earnest, piercing gaze, as if he expected to see the forms of the dreaded Apaches become luminous and reveal themselves in the black night around.

No ray of light relieved the Egyptian blackness. The campfire had been allowed to die out completely, and no red ember, glowering like a demon's eye, showed where it had been. The trained eye might have detected the faintest suspicion of light near the opening overhead, but it was faint indeed.

"They keep together," added Fred to himself, as he distinguished the soft, stealthy tread over the ground. "I should think they would separate, and they would be the more likely to find the place between them; but they want to be together when they run against Mickey, I guess."

The shadowy footsteps were not regular. Occasionally they paused, and then they hurried on again, and then they settled down into the stealthiest kind of movement. The lad, it is true, had the newly found revolver, with several of its chambers loaded, at his command. There was some doubt, however, whether it could be relied upon, owing to the probable length of time that had elapsed since the charges were placed there.

As a precaution, Mickey O'Rooney had placed new caps upon the tubes, but had chosen to leave the charges themselves undisturbed. This beautiful weapon the lad held grasped in his hand, determined to blaze away at the prowling murderers the instant they should reveal themselves with sufficient distinctness to make his shots certain.

An annoying delay followed. The Apaches seemed to know very nearly where the right spot was, without being able to locate it definitely. The footsteps were heard first in one direction and then they changed off to another. The warriors acted precisely as if they knew the location of their intended victims, but were seeking to find whether they were in the right position to be easily attacked.

Lieutenant R. H. Jayne

Thus matters remained for ten or fifteen minutes longer, during which the lad held himself on the alert, and was no little puzzled to comprehend the meaning for the course of their enemies.

"They daren't do anything, now that they know where we are. They're afraid we're on the watch, and think if they wait a while longer, we will drop off to sleep; but they will find—"

A sudden light just then broke in upon young Munson. He was looking off in the direction of the sound, when the phosphorescent gleam of a pair of eyes shot out from the darkness upon him.

There was a greenish glare in the unexpected appearance that left no doubt of their identity. Instead of Indians, as he had imagined at first, there was some kind of a wild animal that was prowling about them. None of the Apaches had entered the cave at all—only a single beast.

But where had he come from? By what means had he entered the cave?

These were very significant questions, of the greatest importance to the two who were shut within the subterranean prison. Fred did not feel himself competent to answer, so he reached over and shook Mickey harder than ever, determined that he should arouse.

"Come, wake up, you sleepy head," he called out. "There might a dozen bears come down on you and eat you up, before you would open your eyes! Come, Mickey, there is need of your waking!"

"Begorrah—but—there's more naad of me slaaping," muttered the Irishman, gradually recalling his senses. "I was in the midst of a beautiful draam, in which there came two lovely females, that looked like Bridget O'Flaherty and Molly McFizzle. Both were smiling in their winsome way on me, and both were advancing to give me a swaat kiss, or a crack over the head, I don't know which, when, just before they raiched me, you sticks out your paw and gives me a big shake. Arrah, ye spalpeen, why did ye do that?"

"Didn't you hear me say there was something in the cavern? I thought there were a couple of Apaches at first, but I guess it is a wild animal."

The Irishman was all attention on the instant, and he started bolt upright.

"Whisht! what's that ye're saying? Will ye plaze say it over again?"

The lad hurriedly told him that an animal of some kind was lurking near them. Mickey caught up his rifle, and demanded to know where he was. In such darkness as enveloped them it was necessary that the eyes of the beast should be at a certain angle in order to become visible to the two watchers. Both heard his light footsteps, and knew where the eyes were likely to be discerned.

"*There he is!*" exclaimed Fred, as he caught sight of the green, phosphorescent glitter of the two orbs, which is peculiar to the eyes of the feline species.

Mickey detected them at the same moment, and drew his rifle to his shoulder. He kept the kneeling position, fearing that the target would vanish if he should wait until he could rise. It is no easy thing for a hunter to take aim when he is utterly unable to detect the slightest portion of his weapon, and it was this fact which caused Mickey to delay his firing.

Lieutenant R. H. Jayne

However, before he could make his aim any way satis-factory, a bright thought struck him, and he lowered his gun, carefully letting the hammer down upon the tube.

"Ain't you going to fire?" asked the lad, who could not understand the delay.

"Whisht, now! would ye have me slay me best friend?"

"I don't understand you, Mickey."

"S'pose I'd shot the baste, whatever he is, that would be the end of him; but lave him alone, and he'll show us the way out."

"How can he do that?"

"Don't you obsarve," said the man, who haf got the theory all perfectly arranged in his mind, "that that creature couldn't get into this cave without coming in some way?"

There was no gainsaying such logic as that, but Fred knew that his friend meant more than he said.

"Of course he couldn't get in here without having some way of doing it. But suppose he took the same means as we did? How is that going to help us?"

But the Irishman was certain that such could not be the case.

"There ain't any wild beasts as big fools as we was. Ye couldnt git 'em to walk into such a hole, any more than ye could git an Irisman to gaze calmly upon a head without hitting it. Ye can make up your mind that there's some way leading into this cavern, which nobody knows anything about, excepting this wild creature, and, if we let him alone, he'll go out again, showing us the path."

"I should think if he knew the route some of the Indians would learn it."

"So anybody would think; but the crayther has not given 'em the chance—so how can they larn it? If we play our cards right, me laddy, we're sure to win."

"What kind of an animal is it?"

They were all the time gazing at the point where the eyes were last seen, but the beast was continually shifting its position, so that the orbs were no longer visible. The faint tipping of his feet upon the gravely earth was heard, and now and then the transient flash of his eyes, as he whisked back and forth, was caught, but all vanished again almost as soon as seen. All that could be learned was, that whatever the species of the animal, he owned large eyes, and they were placed close together. Neither of the two were sufficiently acquainted with the peculiarities of the different animals of the West to identify them by any slight peculiarities.

"I don't think he can be an ilephant or a rhinoceros," said Mickey, reflectively, "because such crathurs don't grow in these parts. What about his being a grizzly bear?"

"He can't be that," said Fred, who had been given time to note the special character of the footsteps before he awoke his companion. "He walks too lightly."

"What do you conclude him to be?"

"If there were such things as wild dogs, I would be sure he was one."

"Then I have it; he must be a wolf."

"I guess you're right. He acts just like one—trotting here and there, while his eyes shine like we used to see them when we were camped on the prairie, and they used to hang round the camp waiting for a chance to get something to eat."

"It's aisy to double him up," said Mickey,who just then caught a glimpse of the eyes again; "but if he'll show the way out of here, I'll make a vow never to shoot another wolf, even if he tries to chaw me head off."

"How are we going to discover the place?"

"Just foller him. He'll hang round a while, very likely all night, and when he finds out there's nothing to make here, he'll trot off agin. All we've got to do is to do the same, and he'll show the way out."

"It don't look so easy to me," said Fred, a few minutes later, while he had been busily turning the scheme over in his mind. "If we only had the daylight to see him, it wouldn't be so hard, but here he is right close to us, and it is only now and then that we can tell where he is."

"Yees are right, for it isn't likely that we can walk right straight out by the way that he does; but we can larn from his movements pretty nearly where the place is, and then we can take a torch and hunt for a day or two, and I don't see how we can miss it."

There seemed to be reason in this, although the lad could not feel as sanguine as did his companion. The wolf, as he believed it to be, was doubtless familiar with every turn of the cave, and, when he was ready to go, was likely to vanish in a twinkling—skurrying away with a speed that would defy pursuit. However, there was a promise, or a possibility, at least, of success, and that certainly was something to be cheerful over, even though the prospect was not brilliant, and Fred was resolved that failure should not come through remissness of his.

Choose from Thousands of 1stWorldLibrary Classics By

A. M. Barnard
Ada Leverson
Adolphus William Ward
Aesop
Agatha Christie
Alexander Aaronsohn
Alexander Kielland
Alexandre Dumas
Alfred Gatty
Alfred Ollivant
Alice Duer Miller
Alice Turner Curtis
Alice Dunbar
Allen Chapman
Alleyne Ireland
Ambrose Bierce
Amelia E. Barr
Amory H. Bradford
Andrew Lang
Andrew McFarland Davis
Andy Adams
Angela Brazil
Anna Alice Chapin
Anna Sewell
Annie Besant
Annie Hamilton Donnell
Annie Payson Call
Annie Roe Carr
Annonaymous
Anton Chekhov
Archibald Lee Fletcher
Arnold Bennett
Arthur C. Benson
Arthur Conan Doyle
Arthur M. Winfield
Arthur Ransome
Arthur Schnitzler
Arthur Train
Atticus
B.H. Baden-Powell
B. M. Bower
B. C. Chatterjee
Baroness Emmuska Orczy
Baroness Orczy
Basil King
Bayard Taylor
Ben Macomber
Bertha Muzzy Bower
Bjornstjerne Bjornson

Booth Tarkington
Boyd Cable
Bram Stoker
C. Collodi
C. E. Orr
C. M. Ingleby
Carolyn Wells
Catherine Parr Traill
Charles A. Eastman
Charles Amory Beach
Charles Dickens
Charles Dudley Warner
Charles Farrar Browne
Charles Ives
Charles Kingsley
Charles Klein
Charles Hanson Towne
Charles Lathrop Pack
Charles Romyn Dake
Charles Whibley
Charles Willing Beale
Charlotte M. Braeme
Charlotte M. Yonge
Charlotte Perkins Stetson
Clair W. Hayes
Clarence Day Jr.
Clarence E. Mulford
Clemence Housman
Confucius
Coningsby Dawson
Cornelis DeWitt Wilcox
Cyril Burleigh
D. H. Lawrence
Daniel Defoe
David Garnett
Dinah Craik
Don Carlos Janes
Donald Keyhoe
Dorothy Kilner
Dougan Clark
Douglas Fairbanks
E. Nesbit
E. P. Roe
E. Phillips Oppenheim
E. S. Brooks
Earl Barnes
Edgar Rice Burroughs
Edith Van Dyne
Edith Wharton

Edward Everett Hale
Edward J. O'Biren
Edward S. Ellis
Edwin L. Arnold
Eleanor Atkins
Eleanor Hallowell Abbott
Eliot Gregory
Elizabeth Gaskell
Elizabeth McCracken
Elizabeth Von Arnim
Ellem Key
Emerson Hough
Emilie F. Carlen
Emily Bronte
Emily Dickinson
Enid Bagnold
Enilor Macartney Lane
Erasmus W. Jones
Ernie Howard Pie
Ethel May Dell
Ethel Turner
Ethel Watts Mumford
Eugene Sue
Eugenie Foa
Eugene Wood
Eustace Hale Ball
Evelyn Everett-green
Everard Cotes
F. H. Cheley
F. J. Cross
F. Marion Crawford
Fannie E. Newberry
Federick Austin Ogg
Ferdinand Ossendowski
Fergus Hume
Florence A. Kilpatrick
Fremont B. Deering
Francis Bacon
Francis Darwin
Frances Hodgson Burnett
Frances Parkinson Keyes
Frank Gee Patchin
Frank Harris
Frank Jewett Mather
Frank L. Packard
Frank V. Webster
Frederic Stewart Isham
Frederick Trevor Hill
Frederick Winslow Taylor

Friedrich Kerst
Friedrich Nietzsche
Fyodor Dostoyevsky
G.A. Henty
G.K. Chesterton
Gabrielle E. Jackson
Garrett P. Serviss
Gaston Leroux
George A. Warren
George Ade
Geroge Bernard Shaw
George Cary Eggleston
George Durston
George Ebers
George Eliot
George Gissing
George MacDonald
George Meredith
George Orwell
George Sylvester Viereck
George Tucker
George W. Cable
George Wharton James
Gertrude Atherton
Gordon Casserly
Grace E. King
Grace Gallatin
Grace Greenwood
Grant Allen
Guillermo A. Sherwell
Gulielma Zollinger
Gustav Flaubert
H. A. Cody
H. B. Irving
H.C. Bailey
H. G. Wells
H. H. Munro
H. Irving Hancock
H. R. Naylor
H. Rider Haggard
H. W. C. Davis
Haldeman Julius
Hall Caine
Hamilton Wright Mabie
Hans Christian Andersen
Harold Avery
Harold McGrath
Harriet Beecher Stowe
Harry Castlemon
Harry Coghill
Harry Houidini

Hayden Carruth
Helent Hunt Jackson
Helen Nicolay
Hendrik Conscience
Hendy David Thoreau
Henri Barbusse
Henrik Ibsen
Henry Adams
Henry Ford
Henry Frost
Henry James
Henry Jones Ford
Henry Seton Merriman
Henry W Longfellow
Herbert A. Giles
Herbert Carter
Herbert N. Casson
Herman Hesse
Hildegard G. Frey
Homer
Honore De Balzac
Horace B. Day
Horace Walpole
Horatio Alger Jr.
Howard Pyle
Howard R. Garis
Hugh Lofting
Hugh Walpole
Humphry Ward
Ian Maclaren
Inez Haynes Gillmore
Irving Bacheller
Isabel Cecilia Williams
Isabel Hornibrook
Israel Abrahams
Ivan Turgenev
J.G.Austin
J. Henri Fabre
J. M. Barrie
J. M. Walsh
J. Macdonald Oxley
J. R. Miller
J. S. Fletcher
J. S. Knowles
J. Storer Clouston
J. W. Duffield
Jack London
Jacob Abbott
James Allen
James Andrews
James Baldwin

James Branch Cabell
James DeMille
James Joyce
James Lane Allen
James Lane Allen
James Oliver Curwood
James Oppenheim
James Otis
James R. Driscoll
Jane Abbott
Jane Austen
Jane L. Stewart
Janet Aldridge
Jens Peter Jacobsen
Jerome K. Jerome
Jessie Graham Flower
John Buchan
John Burroughs
John Cournos
John F. Kennedy
John Gay
John Glasworthy
John Habberton
John Joy Bell
John Kendrick Bangs
John Milton
John Philip Sousa
John Taintor Foote
Jonas Lauritz Idemil Lie
Jonathan Swift
Joseph A. Altsheler
Joseph Carey
Joseph Conrad
Joseph E. Badger Jr
Joseph Hergesheimer
Joseph Jacobs
Jules Vernes
Julian Hawthrone
Julie A Lippmann
Justin Huntly McCarthy
Kakuzo Okakura
Karle Wilson Baker
Kate Chopin
Kenneth Grahame
Kenneth McGaffey
Kate Langley Bosher
Kate Langley Bosher
Katherine Cecil Thurston
Katherine Stokes
L. A. Abbot
L. T. Meade

L. Frank Baum
Latta Griswold
Laura Dent Crane
Laura Lee Hope
Laurence Housman
Lawrence Beasley
Leo Tolstoy
Leonid Andreyev
Lewis Carroll
Lewis Sperry Chafer
Lilian Bell
Lloyd Osbourne
Louis Hughes
Louis Joseph Vance
Louis Tracy
Louisa May Alcott
Lucy Fitch Perkins
Lucy Maud Montgomery
Luther Benson
Lydia Miller Middleton
Lyndon Orr
M. Corvus
M. H. Adams
Margaret E. Sangster
Margret Howth
Margaret Vandercook
Margaret W. Hungerford
Margret Penrose
Maria Edgeworth
Maria Thompson Daviess
Mariano Azuela
Marion Polk Angellotti
Mark Overton
Mark Twain
Mary Austin
Mary Catherine Crowley
Mary Cole
Mary Hastings Bradley
Mary Roberts Rinehart
Mary Rowlandson
M. Wollstonecraft Shelley
Maud Lindsay
Max Beerbohm
Myra Kelly
Nathaniel Hawthrone
Nicolo Machiavelli
O. F. Walton
Oscar Wilde

Owen Johnson
P.G. Wodehouse
Paul and Mabel Thorne
Paul G. Tomlinson
Paul Severing
Percy Brebner
Percy Keese Fitzhugh
Peter B. Kyne
Plato
Quincy Allen
R. Derby Holmes
R. L. Stevenson
R. S. Ball
Rabindranath Tagore
Rahul Alvares
Ralph Bonehill
Ralph Henry Barbour
Ralph Victor
Ralph Waldo Emmerson
Rene Descartes
Ray Cummings
Rex Beach
Rex E. Beach
Richard Harding Davis
Richard Jefferies
Richard Le Gallienne
Robert Barr
Robert Frost
Robert Gordon Anderson
Robert L. Drake
Robert Lansing
Robert Lynd
Robert Michael Ballantyne
Robert W. Chambers
Rosa Nouchette Carey
Rudyard Kipling
Saint Augustine
Samuel B. Allison
Samuel Hopkins Adams
Sarah Bernhardt
Sarah C. Hallowell
Selma Lagerlof
Sherwood Anderson
Sigmund Freud
Standish O'Grady
Stanley Weyman
Stella Benson
Stella M. Francis

Stephen Crane
Stewart Edward White
Stijn Streuvels
Swami Abhedananda
Swami Parmananda
T. S. Ackland
T. S. Arthur
The Princess Der Ling
Thomas A. Janvier
Thomas A Kempis
Thomas Anderton
Thomas Bailey Aldrich
Thomas Bulfinch
Thomas De Quincey
Thomas Dixon
Thomas H. Huxley
Thomas Hardy
Thomas More
Thornton W. Burgess
U. S. Grant
Upton Sinclair
Valentine Williams
Various Authors
Vaughan Kester
Victor Appleton
Victor G. Durham
Victoria Cross
Virginia Woolf
Wadsworth Camp
Walter Camp
Walter Scott
Washington Irving
Wilbur Lawton
Wilkie Collins
Willa Cather
Willard F. Baker
William Dean Howells
William le Queux
W. Makepeace Thackeray
William W. Walter
William Shakespeare
Winston Churchill
Yei Theodora Ozaki
Yogi Ramacharaka
Young E. Allison
Zane Grey